Loveless

Mike McGonigal

continuum

NEW YORK • LONDON

2009

The Continuum International Publishing Group Inc
80 Maiden Lane, New York, NY 10038

The Continuum International Publishing Group Ltd
The Tower Building, 11 York Road, London SE1 7NX

www.continuumbooks.com

Printed in the United States of America

Library of Congress Cataloging-in-Publication Data

McGonigal, Mike.
Loveless / Mike McGonigal.
p. cm. -- (33 1/3)
ISBN-13: 978-0-8264-1548-6 (pbk. : alk. paper)
ISBN-10: 0-8264-1548-2 (pbk. : alk. paper)
1. My Bloody Valentine (Musical group). Loveless.   I. Title.
ML421.M9M34 2006
782.42166092'2--dc22

2006027355

Contents

Disclaimer

Although the members of My Bloody Valentine submitted to interviews for this book, and all the quotes from those interviews contained herein are reasonably correct, this is in no way an official My Bloody Valentine book, and the views expressed (except in direct quotes) belong to the author, and not the band.

Foreword
Slow

Unless otherwise noted, all quotes are from interviews conducted by the author in late 2005 and early 2006. Bilinda Butcher and Kevin Shields were spoken with on the phone, while the other interviews were conducted via email. Vinita Joshi of Rocket Girl helped arrange most of the interviews, and she also kept sending encouraging emails and helpful suggestions. I owe her big time.

Ned Raggett, All Music Guide scribe and the "king" of I Love Music, gave excellent and detailed editing suggestions. I'm grateful to him for sharing his essay on *Loveless* from the book *Marooned* (Da Capo, 2007), prepublication; it's essential reading. Speaking of books, to arrive at a proper timeline for the recording information, I relied quite a bit on David Cavanagh's *The Creation Records Story: My Magpie Eyes Are Hungry for the Prize* (Virgin Books,

2001), my copy of which was borrowed from my ex-housemate, Michael.

David Barker is an amazingly patient and helpful editor. Thank God he is, 'cause it basically took as long to write the thing as it did for the band to record the album (though it cost considerably less money). For transcription assistance and further editing suggestions, I'm indebted to Lucy from Sonic Boom, Philip Pickens, Karl Ivanson, Jennifer O'Connor, Jana Martin, Fred Cisterna, Andrew Pih, Dixie Marco and you if I forgot to mention you and you helped in some way. Thanks also to Douglas Shepherd, Steve Connell, Jason Bokros, Kevin McGonigal, Liz Haley, Tae Won Yu, Eugene Booth, Marilyn McGonigal, Luc Sante, the Sundbys, David Keenan and Jim Wiles.

This book is dedicated to Lily Hudson, because what kind of schmuck doesn't dedicate a book to his girlfriend (especially when she's fiercely smart and puts up with all his crap, yet loves him anyway)? And I know it's cheesy to say it, but this book wouldn't exist without Kevin Shields, one of the smartest and humblest people I've ever had the pleasure to talk to.

Chapter One
You Made Me Realize

Three quarters of the way through a show by My Bloody Valentine at a mid-sized concert hall in 1992 in Pennsylvania, we're all hit by absolutely blinding noise from the stage. My ears need a few seconds to adjust; I can't hear anything at all at first even though I can tell the band is furiously going at it, bent over their instruments as they are. My ears must be so overloaded that nothing registers. It's a vacuum, like in the summer when you come out into the sunlit street after being inside for hours in a dark cafe, when you have to just stand there a few seconds, squinting and blinking dazedly before your eyes allow in this new information—the cars and the people and where the dog shit on the sidewalk might be.

Even the monitor speakers are turned around toward the crowd, turned as high as they'll go, and now I learn what it must be like to stick my head inside of a jet engine. Surprise: it's fucking unbearable. The band had been playing a song a few seconds prior to this barrage—"You Made Me Realize," originally the first tune on their first recording for the Creation label, a five-song EP released on August 8, 1988. The black and white cover showed a pretty woman that I took to be guitarist and vocalist Bilinda Butcher laying down on the grass, her eyes rolled upward, a long knife and flowers placed across her throat, cropped to show just her shoulders and head. It was Goth, but not too Goth because it was hot.

The words to the song, near as I could make them out anyway, seemed pretty typical for the band at the time, and help you respect their decision never to print the lyrics in their records. "What did you say you'd find / Then come, come, come, get the hell inside / You can close your eyes / Well you might as well commit suicide / Wait for me because I waited for you / No that's not what you should do / Don't hate me 'cause I don't hate you / Insane eyes / You made me realize" This is not a band you listen to because you love their lyrics, since the way they sing them is so low in the mix—not to mention how daft they are. We'll briefly return to the issue of MBV's lyrics and why songs with words you can't really understand are so often superior later on.

"You Made Me Realize" is among My Bloody Valentine's most thrashy, headbangy numbers, but it's definitely a song nonetheless—you know, verse, chorus, verse.

And yet, what is happening now, in the concert hall, sounds like what your parents think you listen to: pure noise; there appear to be no dynamics to it at all. It sounds dreadful. It is can't-think-straight loud, a deliriously loud kind of loud. It seems to be tacky, showoffy, offensive and most of all, really painful. Not to play the indie rock version of "Quien Es Más Macho?" with you or anything, but I'd seen some very loud shows—Hüsker Dü, Motörhead, Gen Ken, Black Flag, you get the drift.

The thing is, I knew (or should have known) to expect this. When we were in the car en route, my friends Rusty and Mark had even bet each other about how long "it" would be tonight. This was something the band was already renowned for, this noise stretch inside of "You Made Me Realize." I just hadn't really paid attention, I guess. Rusty and Mark were waiters at Cafe Orlin in the East Village who, along with several other Orlin staff, later wound up working for Matador Records—Rusty as national sales director, Mark as bassist for the Dustdevils and then Pavement. Rabid music geeks with acute social skills, they were friends with the band and the reason I'd driven out all this way, my ride being exchanged for entrance and the chance to pal around backstage afterward.

Loveless had been released a few months before, and My Bloody Valentine was now my favorite band. They were at this point pretty much everyone I knew's favorite band, so of course I was there. I'd seen them in '89, before I was much of a convert, at the behest of the Orlin crew. That entire show at the comparatively tiny club Maxwell's in Hoboken, New Jersey, had been so loud (with J. Mascis from Dinosaur Jr. manning the soundboard that night) that we essentially watched the show from the room next door, it being more than loud enough through soundproofed concrete. But if they'd played the noise bit that time, I can't say.

Here, tonight, the group has far more power going for them than they did at Maxwell's. And they are using it, all of it. I am feeling very nostalgic for Maxwell's, wishing I could slip away easily. I'm smack in the middle of a large, confused crowd. People are freaking the fuck out from the noise, making for the exits or doing that swarm-dance version of slam-dancing that larger venues and alternative rock bands both tend to coax from younger audiences. Lots of these kids look really young, and do not look happy. I feel like maybe I could be sick, for real, so I step back from the swirl of backward baseball caps, my pulse quickening.

I can imagine this all is coming across as hyper-hyperbolic, but the sounds feel like they are hitting me, especially in the stomach; it's truly like getting socked in the gut. I recall a concert by the band Flipper in 1984, in Miami, when my friend Malcolm Tent had animatedly informed me not to eat anything before that gig. He said the bassist deliberately detuned his bass to a really low frequency that was supposed to trigger audience members' bowels to let loose, creating potentially the exact reversal of a G.G. Allin show. That turned out to be bogus, but I was really scared the whole time Flipper played and was super afraid I'd accidentally shit myself at this cool punk rock concert I'd snuck into, at the age of sixteen.

Later, at NYU as an undergrad, I researched experiments supposedly conducted during WWII by the British Army into the efficacy of sound as an instrument of war. I learned that "sonic cannons" had apparently been constructed at some point, and of course tested on Army personnel. Throbbing Gristle had done a lot of research into this stuff too, apparently. As I'm pummeled by these sounds I wonder if they hadn't somehow gotten hold of one of these things, and now have one pointed straight at us.

Somehow, though (and it's really hard to say how or exactly when, though I'd say at least five minutes in), things start to change, and the sounds become less intense—or less threatening, more organic and almost melodic—and my stomach's fine. The crowd of kids toward the front who'd started to thrash about uncontrollably are still moving, but with less menace. They move slowly and lurchingly, like drugged livestock. Perhaps it's that my ears have adjusted to the pain? Or maybe they've shut down entirely, and what I'm "hearing" are the increasingly pleasant, ringing tones of endorphin rush?

Now, just as suddenly as it hit in the first place, something truly beautiful is happening. A playful array of overtones can be heard bouncing about on top of the dirge.

Everything goes into slow motion. I am absolutely transported and it seems that this cloud of harmonics sweetly filling the room, these delightful ping-ponging notes, are perhaps the whole point of this exercise, what the band had been trying to get to all along. The band do not appear to have changed what they're doing, they're still furiously playing what appears to be one chord, all of them. I glance, nervously, animatedly about the room to see if other people have "gotten it" or not. Some cute girls are hippie dancing now to this sustained barrage, so yeah I think they have.

There is a shimmering, hallucinatory quality to these notes that dance atop the noise, and it's hard to explain—nor have I found it to be captured on tape after scouring live shows. At best you might hear a faint Xerox of a Xerox similar to the way Charlie Patton's recordings show you maybe one tenth of what he was doing with his guitar. But anyway, you want to know what it sounded like? If you played Lou Reed's *Metal Machine Music* album and the middle ten minutes of Terry Riley's *Rainbow in Curved Air* at the same time, well, that would probably sound like shit. But if you can imagine what that might sound like if it didn't sound like shit, a heavy duty industrial dirge with bliss-drone birdcalls atop it, then you'd have a good estimate. It was brutally psychedelic, and more than mildly euphoric.

Since that concert, I've had similar sensations briefly occur at performances by La Monte Young, Maryanne Amacher, the Sun City Girls, and a few sacred harp singings in East Tennessee—like there is a ghost of the music you are witnessing riding on top of it, or inside of it, that your body is somehow a vessel for total sonic bliss. I've never experienced the sensation so intensely, or so violently, before or since, even when seeing MBV do the same thing two other times on that tour.

That night, the show is over for me as soon as the band goes back into the lurching chug-chug-changa-chung, chug-chug-changa-chung chord progression of the song to close it out. I am in a daze, trying to figure out what just happened, wondering idly if it was worth the hearing loss. I have questions: Why did it take several minutes of excruciating noise before I could begin to hear these lovely, ethereal counternotes happening inside of it? Was it just a question of adjustment, or hallucination, or did it take that long for them to appear? Was that really one of the best times I'd ever felt in my life, and why?

Driving home afterward, I have this vague suspicion that the seemingly painstaking *Loveless*, a record instantly rumored to have cost a bazillion dollars and to have bankrupted its record label and known to have taken years to record, was somehow inspired by the noise section of "You Made Me Realize," as if *Loveless* itself, with all its smeared melodies and ghostly ethereal feedback, were the controlled symphonic version of this cruder and more spontaneous freak-out experiment. It will take me almost fourteen years to ask guitarist Kevin Shields about the rela-

tionship between the two, talking on the phone just before
Christmas 2005, and he basically laughs at me when I do,
sweetly taking me to task for trying to read too much into
things. Perhaps my visceral, disoriented response to this
section of their live show had so closely mirrored my ini-
tial response to hearing the album, where I felt as if I'd
been suspended upside down in a tank filled with beautiful
tropical fish, that it only made sense that I ended up con-
flating the two?

In 2004, the webzine *Buddyhead* printed an interview
with Shields where he reminisced at length about the
"noise" bit. "Usually people would experience a type of
sensory deprivation, and they would lose the sense of time.
It would force them to be in the moment, and since people
don't usually get to experience that, there'd be a sense of ela-
tion. There would be a feeling of, "Wow, that was really
weird, I don't know what happened, but I suddenly heard
this symphony . . . " It was such a huge noise with so much
texture to it, it allowed people to imagine anything. Like
when you hypnotize somebody, and nothing becomes
something. That was what the whole purpose became."

It's both a revelation and a letdown to read Shields say
this. It validates what I had heard, in a way, but it also made
it seem like just some apparition. I want Kevin to say that
the piece had been a mathematically derived bliss-through-
pain formula, a Tony Conrad or Henry Flynt–like controlled research approach with sine waves and amplitudinal

graphs and frequency ratios painstakingly figured out beforehand, perhaps with a little sacred geometry/harmony of the spheres huzzah thrown in for good measure. And here he's saying it was just a lucky mistake the band hit on one night out of drunken frustration with their audience? And I mean, "When nothing becomes something"? Dude, that sounds like a quote from Baba Ram Dass's *Be Here Now*.

Still curious what the band was doing exactly during "Realize," and where all that melody came from, I press him about it. "There was no melody!," he exclaims. "Every melody everyone had was in their head." The group played "all the strings on the bass at the same time and then me with this whammy pedal able to go two octaves lower and then bring it up and down like that. And then with various distortion pedals I could change the texture of the noise whenever I wanted so it wasn't just like one sound, it was just sort of moving along somehow. It was the best part of the night always and each night it was an experiment to see how long it would take for the audience to turn from like one state to another. A certain percent of the audience would start sticking their fingers up at us or they would put their hands up in the air with their eyes closed, or do something or do something physical. I pretty much would always go on as long as it took to change the audience."

"When it was clear that the audience was changed, totally—even if it was one person left with their fingers in the air or in their ears, we would wait for them to give into it," Kevin explains. "Sometimes it would take forty minutes for that one individual to give up. When the audience was fully and utterly done, we had the signal process where I would look at Debbie and we'd go back into the final parts of the song. That's something we could only do when we did, 'cause now we've all got various accumulated ear damage and other conditions. I'm definitely in the future not going to do experiments like that. The sound of clacking plates really hurts my ears now."

After the Pennsylvania show, I get to hang with the band thanks to the Orlins, and I nervously ask Kevin and drummer Colm O'Coisig if I can release a seven-inch single that would consist solely of the jet engine part from "Realize," as this had never been documented. The break in the studio version only lasts fifteen seconds total and there had never been an official live release by the group, not even one song. They both like the idea, and say "Yes!" and we exchange information. Releasing this record will be a highlight of my life, I think, while I'm leaving the large concrete structure with my friends.

At the time, I edited a fanzine called *Chemical Imbalance* that had seven-inch records with each issue. They'd always been compilations that I assembled by asking people for unreleased material. The MBV single would be the first time that one band alone would appear on one of these records, but I figured it would be worth bending the "rules" a little for my favorite band. Kevin agrees to go back home and listen to the live DAT recordings after the US tour is over, and to excerpt the very best seven to twelve minutes for a release. Months pass and I don't hear from him, until finally, after pestering Kevin on the phone time and again, he informs me that, after listening back to all of the tapes, none of them sound quite good enough. I wonder if he was surprised that the overtone sonata stuff could not be discerned on the recordings? I didn't press him on it, and he was really sweet and apologetic and maybe embarrassed even. It was impossible to be too upset.

Years later, I realize that I've had the very same experience that almost anyone who's attempted since *Loveless* to release music by My Bloody Valentine has had. And all I was personally out was the cost of a few transatlantic phone calls! By 1992, Kevin had seemingly become such a control freak that almost nothing would live up to his standards ever again. Sure, there would be two cover songs recorded by the group, Kevin would keep busy with remixes, and by playing in someone else's rock band, and even record a few sappy songs for a Hollywood movie by himself. But the principal sound of My Bloody Valentine since 1992 has been silence. I come here to praise *Loveless* and not to play the part of the pissed-off fanboy who's still upset that its successor never materialized. I'm not sure I'd want to hear the successor, anyway. And as you'll see, it's even a wonder that *Loveless* ever happened in the first place.

Chapter Two
Loveless

How about a quick tour of the record itself before we get too far into all this?

The cover is a blurry and oversaturated detail of a Fender Jazzmaster. It's a still from Angus Cameron's video for track four, "To Here Knows When," which had been the first song on the Tremolo EP. Neither the band name nor the record title, both in lower case, are easily legible, printed as they are in a vaguely purpley red against a vaguely purpley pink.

Track 1 "Only Shallow" (Butcher, Shields—4:17)

It's ironic that a burst of drums is the first thing you hear on the first song on *Loveless*. Because after two seconds, the drums fade into the background for the rest of the song, and for much of the album, until the final song, the dance-floor-ready "Soon." This one is an overpowering yet light track. A lumbering wall of sound hits at once, guitars woozily caressing each other. The bass kicks in and surges pretty wildly during the bridge to this midtempo tune, while the lyrics are sung in a breathy, beautiful and indecipherable half-asleep whisper that floats atop it all. There is so much going on in the midrange with this song, and the entire album in fact, that to make the slightest change on an equalizer is to drastically alter the sound of it. After hearing *Loveless* first on a boombox and then my stereo, I was struck by how different it sounded depending on where and how you listened to it, so I dorkily carried it around with me for a month to play it on different friends' stereos. We'd sit there, enraptured. "Only Shallow" is powered by what sounds like a broken air raid siren for the hook; it's like getting hit over the head by a lead pillow.

Track 2 "Loomer" (Butcher, Shields—2:38)

After a brief ambient outro from "Only Shallow," we're treated to what might be the best song on the album. A squall of lovely, feeding back guitar lines, beautiful synthy notes and a submerged but groovy vocal are all there, barely audible in the background below layers of gorgeously gliding guitars. Trying to tell what's going on in this song is nearly impossible. Everything sounds ghostly and bright at the same time. It's the sonic equivalent of one of those later period Gerhard Richter paintings, from when he was building up gorgeous layers of paint and then removing them by sanding it all down. I was starting to do a lot of drugs when this record came out, speedballs mostly. You know when the guitars come crashing through right at the start, with the looped feedback lines sort of singing along together? That's exactly how I felt for ten minutes every day, before I fell asleep or reached for more stuff to sell to go cop more (cue the after school special).

Track 3 "Touched" (O'Ciosoig— :56)

Colm's major contribution to the album—a strange and squiggly sampler exercise—may be under a minute, but it's the most futuristic and fucked-up sounding thing on here. It's kind of a shortened extension of the wordless, cacophonous piece "Glider," off the *Glider* EP. I have a friend who swears this song is "the key" to the album. And while I'm not really sure what she means, Ned Raggett suggests that it's where everything becomes transcendently vague, as it's the only tune with no words at all.

Track 4 "To Here Knows When" (Butcher, Shields—5:31)

Here's your dessert, a bit early in the meal but we're not sticklers for convention, are we? There's this constantly surging/receding quality to the distorting guitar drones in the background. It vaguely recalls the start to the Who's "Armenia City in the Sky."

Track 5 "When You Sleep" (Shields—4:11)

The most "normal" (and easily covered) tune on here, and the one that you can just picture all the soon-to-be-rich-and-famous alt-rock bands of the 90s cherry picking from.

Track 6 "I Only Said" (Shields—5:34)

Horror vacui. That's what guys in white suits like to call art that obsessively fills in every nook and cranny of available space. It's often used to describe the visual work of self-taught visionaries such as Adolf Wolfli, Madge Gill and Chris Hipkiss, but it surely applies to these whirlwind four and a quarter minutes as well. This song has a squiggly hook that's not aged so well after thousands of listens. It sort of makes me feel sick to my stomach, to be honest. There's also too much information to take in at once. I need some rest; maybe sort of a rock song, please?

Track 7 "Come in Alone" (Shields—3:58)

And here we go with a sort of rock song/ballady piece, the third most regular tune of the disc. You've got to be careful when writing or talking about this record. Once you give into it, you start believing it's the most transcendent record ever, or one of 'em anyway, and this too easily leads you to believe that it's suddenly okay to relate the album to all the most transcendent experiences in your own life, from your own super cool drug use to your sexual exploits to the way that as a kid you absolutely adored the feeling when part of you feels like it is still moving but the rest of you is still, like when you swim in the ocean then you feel wobbly for half an hour afterward. How you really dug swimming and being on the swings pushing as high as possible, because those were the closest things you could find to flying. Really, it's too easy for this album to turn you into a pretentious twat. Be very careful!!!

Track 8 "Sometimes" (Shields—5:19)

This is the song that sounds the most like ye olde "Sunny Sundae Smile"–era Valentines, all pretty singing over gently strummed guitar. The percussion is a thumping beat that sounds like a helicopter preparing for takeoff, or your heart when it's under duress. Unlike most acoustic/strummy tunes, much of the song happens in the middle and lower ranges of the spectrum. It's brilliant.

Track 9 "Blown a Wish" (Butcher, Shields—3:36)

This song is the cheeriest and among the most heavily dependent on sound washes. It's probably the least "cluttered" song on the record, and the one with the vocals the most foregrounded. It's the only thing MBV ever did that really reminds me of cocktail lounge music, as it almost seems a woozy, futuristic update of the Fifth Dimension, what with all the little vocal blips and blops.

Track 10 "What You Want" (Shields—5:33)

Uptempo and happening mostly in the treble range, this is the song that really makes you jump out of your seat if you don't forget to turn it down a little bit before it gets going. I should point out that this is one of those records arranged like a record; each side progresses very similarly, as if they're mirrors of each other. If you listen closely during the last minute of the song, as the one phrase repeats over and over, there is a bunch of rumbly stuff underneath it that sounds like ghosts fucking, or maybe it's the sound of them ordering takeout but played backward. I hope it's a Satanic message and I've been brainwashed!

Track 11 "Soon" (Shields—6:58)

This was the song that sounded the most from-the-future of the bunch when *Loveless* was released, and today it's likely the most dated, due to how reliant it is on foregrounding the programmed drums. The obvious hit single, and the song that weathered a remix by Andrew Weatherall, it's long and joyous, an excellent melding of dance and alt-rock. If only "baggy"/"Madchester" music sounded like this! I really wanted it to. In case you were wondering, it's perfectly OK to dance like a drunk hippie to this song.

Chapter Three
Paint a Rainbow

In the beginning, Dublin-based My Bloody Valentine brought together the least interesting elements of the Cramps, Joy Division and the Birthday Party. They were derivatively boring, which suited them as they'd named themselves after a dreadful, Canadian knockoff from 1981 of the movie *Friday the 13th*. "The name was thanks to our singer, Dave Stelfox; we'd had much worse names in mind before him, like the Burning Peacocks!" Kevin Shields explains. Stelfox was a camp-loving psychobilly-ish lead singer, and I hear tell he was a super sweet guy and a charismatic lead singer live. The early records that he sings on, and that his girlfriend Tina plays keyboards on in lieu of bass, are pretty awful, however.

To me, this is a big deal, and I tried to think of another band that went from sucking so incredibly hard to being so flat-out great, and I couldn't come up with one. Early, early Sonic Youth is pretty bad but you can tell they know it; it's bad in an art way and besides, those folks had already made good music elsewhere. Most musicians don't start out so excellent or interesting, of course, and whether you're the Meat Puppets or Kinski or Jolie Holland, the template's the same: you begin with borrowed ideas, you work through them, you come up with your own sound in the process somehow, and if you're lucky it doesn't suck too much. In a weird way, MBV can give every embarrassingly banal artist in the world hope that maybe, deep inside them, the egg of genius lies there, dormant and unfertilized. Of course it's likely a very false hope, but call me a romantic.

Shields was born in Queens, New York, and lived on Long Island until he was ten, and when his family moved back to Ireland in 1973 he fell in love with the sound of glam on the radio: the energy, androgyny and otherworldly production style was greatly appealing to him. A few years later he heard the Ramones and fell in love again. Seeing them play on the TV, as he told *Buddyhead*, he "realized [Johnny] wasn't playing guitar—he was generating the sound . . . it was just a noise generator! He was doing what he had to do to make that, but there was no 'playing guitar' involved, you know what I mean?" Kevin and Colm O'Coisog met in Dublin when Kevin was sixteen and Colm fourteen. They became fast friends and were briefly in a punk rock band called the Complex. Later they met

Dave and formed MBV. There weren't a lot of bands in Dublin at the time and the Valentines did do well within the small scene there, but there was no way to be much of a self-supporting band in Dublin at the time.

Gavin Friday, leader of the Virgin Prunes—one of the only interesting acts around—suggested they try their luck overseas. Without really knowing the band's music, he gave them contacts that landed them a show in Holland and hooked them up in Berlin, where they squatted and made their first record, *This Is Your Bloody Valentine*. Moving to London, they began to discard the overt Goth influence on *Geek* and a twelve-inch EP from 1986 called *The New Record by My Bloody Valentine*, which showed a distinct Jesus and Mary Chain influence. After Tina had split the band once *Geek* was finished, Debbie Googe was brought in on bass. Deb explains that an ex-girlfriend of hers named Annie Lloyd was living in Berlin when MBV had been over there. "Annie was a singer in a band called Leningrad Sandwich and she just met them because the Berlin underground scene was pretty small," she says. "And I think the guy that managed her band was involved in putting out the first MBV record. They told her they were moving to London and asked if she knew anyone who could play bass, so she gave them my number. It's amazing I ever joined really, as it was Colm who rang and he has quite a strong Irish accent. The person who took the message was German, and by the time I got it, it made no sense at all. Luckily,

Colm's number got written down, so I just rang it even though I had absolutely no idea who it was. Colm asked me down to a rehearsal, and I went along and then to another, and another. They never actually said I was in the band; they just kept arranging practices and I kept going along."

Bilinda Butcher had been introduced to the group via her boyfriend, who let her know when Dave Conway left and Kevin decided to try lead vocals that there was an opening in the group for a backing vocalist. Already a fan, she was nervous and terrified. "I think probably I was probably scared of Debbie as well, because once I was in her way while she was trying to get her bass cabinet out and I felt a bit nervous about meeting her." Bilinda quickly endeared herself to Debbie, though, when she sang an obscure Dolly Parton tune, "Bargain Store," at the tryouts. It didn't hurt that Bilinda had an old rundown ambulance that was helpful in carting equipment off to gigs, either. Having fully ditched the Cramps/Birthday Party shtick with *Sunny Sundae Smile*, MBV quickly became a half-decent band. Two mini-albums from 1987, *Ecstasy* and *Strawberry Wine* (later collected as *Ecstasy and Wine*), marked a definite, and much-needed, turning point. Their music was now a rarefied, effete and poppy approach to Byrdsian rock: jingle jangle mourning.

Chapter Four
We're So Beautiful

Creation Records was started with a bank loan of a thousand pounds in 1984 by a flashy young Glaswegian named Alan McGee, along with his band mate Dick Green and a guy named Joe Foster who'd cofounded the shambling and often brilliant late 70s act the Television Personalities. Around the same time, McGee started a club called the Living Room, on London's Tottenham Court Road. It was small, but instantly successful. The label itself was named after one of the coolest and most unsung British bands of the 60s. Along with the Who and Monks, the Creation happened to be early experts at a semicontrolled manipulation of feedback. And just in case no one got the reference, McGee's own, pleasantly mediocre act Biff Bang Pow! was named for a tune of theirs.

The label released some of the best chiming guitar rock

of the day: the Loft, the Pastels, Felt, Phil Wilson, Moodists, Jasmine Minks, Nikki Sudden and later Teenage Fanclub. Creation hit it pretty big with their twelfth single, by a band called the Jesus and Mary Chain. That single, the overpowering and druggy buzzsaw pop manifesto "Upside Down" b/w a sloppy, noisy take on an obscure Syd Barrett cover, "Vegetable Man," is one of the greatest debuts in British pop music, and was clearly a big influence on MBV. The band's notoriously loud, short (under ten minutes!) gigs caused riots almost each time, and as they were also good-looking lads in leather and sunglasses, the press couldn't get enough of them. The group quickly signed to Warner, keeping McGee on as their manager, and the ensuing salary helped keep the label afloat. Later in the decade, McGee foresaw the rise of the Manchester indie dance/ acid house scenes, and had more hits with the likes of Primal Scream. In a remarkable third act, McGee signed Oasis and helped to launch Britpop onto the world in the early to mid 1990s.

My Bloody Valentine got paired with Biff Bang Pow! at a gig in Kent, in January of 1988. According to *The Creation Records Story: My Magpie Eyes Are Hungry for the Prize* by David Cavanagh, "that night, McGee and Green stood at the front to watch [MBV], trying to reconcile the indie joke band of yore with the pummeling monster howling before them." As further related in Magpie, McGee then turned to Dick, exclaimed that they'd found the British Hüsker

Dü, and before the night was through the group had decided to record a single for Creation in an inexpensive studio in Walthamstow, east London. Five songs were recorded in less than a week; they were driving, heavy and wonderful. McGee and crew released them all as the "You Made Me Realize" EP. The record was very well received by the press across the board, a first for the band. (Note to Anglophiles and Anglopeeps: I'm aware it was actually released as the "You Made Me Realise" EP, but if I slide down that slippery slope, I'll start spelling color with a "u" in it, and that just doesn't float with my American sensibility, sorry.)

Creation employee number four, Edward Ball, another founding member of the Television Personalities (along with vocalist/songwriter Dan Treacy, who never worked for Creation), recalls meeting the iconoclastic McGee in the early 80s. "We first met around the time the TV Personalities and [Ball's other band] the Times became two separate entities," Ball says, "Dan and I no longer playing in each others bands but meeting up to compare notes. He'd mentioned Alan, and how the TVPs had played his club the Living Room. Then I met Alan, and was so impressed with his enthusiasm! The Times played the Living Room too, and we remained acquaintances through the early 80s but lost contact during the Mary Chain years."

Ball got back in touch with McGee just as the label had signed MBV and was hiring its first "real" employees. "I'd run into Alan at a TVPs gig at the 100 Club in London, and he asked me to make an album for Creation. Not long after that, he extended a job offer to me. Creation at this time was literally just Alan and Dick Green." As the label grew, Alan continued to hire musicians. "Practically all were united by two common factors—that we were musicians and that we were trusted friends of Alan. As the first employee through the door, I was the goodwill guy who communicated with distributor Rough Trade's sales people. As the label's profile built, particularly in the early 90s, I was appointed label spokesman, sort of Derek Taylor to Alan's Beatles, if you will."

Ball's first time seeing MBV was at a pub in North London. "They were the first Creation band I saw in a work capacity," he says. "I was stunned by how brilliant they were. I was first drawn to Colm, like Squiddly Diddley treated with a blurring agent. Then it became apparent that Kevin was the Guv'nor and that they were lifeline dynamic. Along with Debbie's elfin Grim Reaper with the Scything Bass and the slo-mo demure beauty of Belinda, I was sold on the Valentines."

As a kid in South Florida, I personally was super lucky that the guy who ordered imports and indies for the local cool record shop (Bill Ashton at Yesterday & Today) scoured all three British weeklies to discern which of the twenty-eight new bands getting promoted as "brilliant" that week might actually be decent. Ashton had uncanny taste, and thanks to him I was soon picking up all the

Creation releases as they came out, even dreadful ones by the Legend and Les Zarjaz. The funny thing is that by the time MBV signed to Creation in 1988, I was up in New York City pretending to attend college, and hardly paying attention to British music any longer. From my own, myopic point of view (which I didn't know yet to term "rockist") much of the British indie scene in the mid to late 80s was too Gothy and serious, or else too dancey and not serious enough. Thanks to this bias, it took several mix tapes from the Orlins to get me interested in the Valentines in time to pick up the heavy and excellent *Feed Me With Your Kiss* EP and then their 1988 album *Isn't Anything*.

The album was a complete surprise to almost everyone. MBV were progressing incredibly quickly at this point. They were suddenly conversant enough with the genres they had previously borrowed limply from to mix and match at will. It's stunning rock and roll music. And it's amazingly smart in the way it foregrounds feedback as texture, but it totally rocks. It's in many ways more accessible than *Loveless*, largely because if you've never heard it, you kind of have, in the dozens and dozens of other bands who themselves borrowed very heavily from it. I was super psyched at the time, as, while everyone and their mother adored the direction Sonic Youth had taken with *Daydream Nation*, I found it a tad boring in comparison to their previous few. With *Isn't Anything*, I had a new favorite band. It was tough to fathom how they could top it.

Chapter Five
Glider

The British press invented the term "shoegazer" in the late 80s to describe certain loud and fuzzily melodic bands' "motionless performing style, where they stood on stage and stared at the floor," to quote All Music Guide. Like grunge, it's one of those half-derogatory phrases that struck a chord, and then stuck for good. According to online dictionary Wikipedia, "*Isn't Anything* by My Bloody Valentine, released in 1988, is said to have defined the sound," which is to say that most shoegazing bands took at least part of MBV's big rock approach and ran with it. Which part did they take? For the most part, they borrowed wholesale that hard-edged swooning sound, the weird and time-slowing trick of bending a detuned Barre chord in and out of tune.

"I can play almost anything if I really want to," Shields

says, then instantly contradicts himself with, "it's just that I haven't a talent to be a flashy guitar player. Rhythmically, I can play more like Johnny Ramone than Jimi Hendrix. Texture comes through rhythm, it comes through and the audience perceives it as just a sound. The basic thing is using chord structures with open strings and different weird tunings, combined with a guitar [going through] a Vox amplifier. That amp has the capacity to play almost anything through it, plus it reproduces the sound of the weird chords very well, where Fenders and Marshalls don't." The gimmick appeared to spread as fast as drugs, from first generation British acts like Swervedriver, Ride, Moose and Catherine Wheel to their arguably more musically interesting American offspring the Lilys and Swirlies. "But all those bands as far as I know actually used choruses, pedals and flangers," Shields explains. "No other band played that guitar like me. No one used the tremolo arm aside from us. We did everything solely with the tremolo arm; it's such a weird modification. It's difficult to do, and also so obvious, so no one else did that."

"I just kind of found my own way, and my own feel, my own way of playing. I found that if there was only one guitar track whilst the vocals were going, split between different amps and mics, the sound was bigger, especially when you use open strings and tunings and the tremolo arm on Jazzmasters or Jaguars. I didn't have to consciously think about it; I was able to express this constant feeling of expression. It's hard to explain the sound of the guitar bending. What you hear is what it is *between* the sound, with the open tunings and the guitar bending." Shields didn't invent this technique; half a dozen really cool songs touched upon this effect rather swimmingly, by artists as diverse as the Kinks, Who, Talking Heads and even early alt-country rockers Green on Red. I should also mention that similar techniques had been employed by any number of shimmery 60s surf bands.

"The very first time in my life I did that sound," Kevin says, "that bending guitar sound with a whole chord bending at once—was on 'Slow,' in 1988, from the 'You Made Me Realize' EP. That session was written and recorded in five days, all on borrowed equipment, including a Jazzmaster with a tremolo arm." Kevin was aware that J. Mascis from Dinosaur Jr. used the same guitar. He had one himself, "a copy," but his didn't have the tremolo arm. "It didn't come with one so I never thought about it," he says. "I was totally into Dinosaur Jr. by the time we were on Creation. But I had always been a big Birthday Party fan and Rowland Howard played a Jaguar, so that was a big influence; I always wanted one. And Sonic Youth played them too, so I was really into them."

I don't know too much about guitars, but as a little bit of a fanboy myself, it makes me giddy to hear Kevin speak so reverently of his American guitar gods, as if that makes us both part of the same club. Similarly, Shields doesn't seem to feel proprietary ownership over his bent guitar shtick, and is eager to talk of searching for other examples that predate his own use of it. He considers a key element of the method to be "the mentality of bending as a hook line." Shields credits dance music as an influence here, with its elastic melody lines driven by bendy pitch wheels. As to Green on Red's own warped guitar song, Shields says that "if you hear it you're gonna go, 'Fucking hell!' You are going to think that we would have heard that. And we could have, subconsciously. The whole rest of [Green on Red's] repertoire is nothing like that. But this one track had this kind of melody going over the top to the tune of the song, and he started messing with the tremolo arm. He probably only did it through one tenth of the song properly, but he explored it within that song." Shields opines that it's "a wonderful example of how if the universe is one entity, and it tries ideas out—and goes 'This is a really cool idea, but this person isn't the right person to be doing it because they've got other things to be doing.'"

"It's really hard to do unless you set the guitar up in a very specific way," Shields says. "I modified all the tremolo arms. I never did it with stock position. If you do it normally, it doesn't work at all. The bending has a quality that is universal, it's in all cultures. It's something that just got a little bit wiped out of Western music for a while." When applied with some kind of skill, this very act of boing-oing-oing-ing the strings helps bring rock/pop music closer to any number of musical traditions that exist outside of the twelve-note scale, from Indian classical to the "blue" notes of American vernacular sound, or even twenty-first century classical "just intonation" music, as long as we're leaping about. Undoubtedly exposure to the alternate tunings of Sonic Youth played a role in opening Shields's ears to such possibilities. Those guys had themselves apprenticed with "rocking minimalist" masters such as Rhys Chatham, Arnold Dreyblatt and Glenn Branca to arrive at their signature, screwdrivers-jammed-into-the-fretboard approach.

But it seems that Shields was born with an interest in slight modulations in phasing and variations in slightly "off" notes. My favorite anecdote about Kevin from David Cavanagh's book is related by *Loveless* engineer Alan Moulder. According to him, a very young Kevin would often sit down in the kitchen with his little sister, Ann Marie, the both of them humming one note, for a really long time. "And then he'd slightly take it out of tune so that the notes would modulate and drive his parents crazy. That was at *four!*," he's quoted as saying. Anyone who's ever listened to La Monte Young's *Theater of Eternal Music* will dig how deep this kind of activity can be. (I think when I was four, I'd recently discovered how to pick my nose, and that I liked Batman.)

"Normally when people use a tremolo arm, you can hear them bending it, going up and down," Kevin says. "For me, it was making it sound sort of unconscious, so that it didn't sound like someone was doing it. It wasn't intellectual. It was more that I had a feeling, and I discovered through the tremolo arm that I could express it. That's all. My frustration of not being able to express myself with a guitar—properly, physically—was suddenly gone, and I could be totally expressive. It's controlled not consciously but not subconsciously. It ebbs and flows. It can be taught, as well. I taught Bilinda from scratch and she was quite good at it; she didn't know any other way of playing guitar."

Kevin brings another North American guitar god into the picture, noting that "for Neil Young, having the tremolo arm in his hand is a major part of his technique. I was definitely more from the Neil Young school—where it's making the texture way bigger. That's why his guitar is so massive. But he does it really subtly—that way he opens the sound up. And I didn't even know Neil Young did it until much later. It makes you perceive it twice as big as it really is 'cause the frame of reference is twice as much as it was. Because the pitch is twice as much information and the tonality is twice as much information. So your brain goes, 'This is big, this is more than one guitar.' You know what I mean?" By the time he got to the dense soup of *Loveless*, Shields says that "People were just like 'That's millions of guitars playing!' People were thinking it's hundreds of guitar tracks, when it's actually got less guitar tracks than most people's demo tapes have."

Chapter Six
Only Shallow

Here's a list of possible antecedents for *Loveless*: a bakers' dozen, mostly slow and dreamy, "pop"-based musical works which are equal parts raw invention and delightful melody, and that predate *Loveless*. (It's a bit wanky, but it was fun to compile—and everyone loves lists, don't they?)

1. Eno, "Needles in the Camel's Eye," off *Here Come the Warm Jets* (EG, 1974)

2. Terry Riley, *Poppy Nogood and the Phantom Band* (Cortical, recorded in 1968 and released in 1997)

3. Faust, "Krautrock" off *Faust IV* (Virgin Rcords, 1973)

4. The self-titled, first Ash Ra Tempel album (Ohr, 1971)

5. Jesus & Mary Chain, "Never Understand" (Creation, 1985)

6. Sonic Youth, "Shadow of a Doubt," from *EVOL* (SST, 1986)

7. Spacemen Three, "Ecstasy in Slow Motion," off of *Dreamweapon: An Evening of Contemporary Sitar Music* (released 1990, Fierce)

8. Arthur Russell, "You Can Make Me Feel Bad," from *Calling Out of Context* (Audika, recorded sometime in the 80s and released in 2004)

9. The Red Krayola, "Transparent Radiation," taken from *Parable of Arable Land* (International Artists, 1967)

10. White Noise, *An Electric Storm* (Island, 1969)

11. Byrds, "5D (Fifth Dimension)," from the record *Fifth Dimension* (Columbia, 1966)

12. Hüsker Dü, "Reoccurring Dreams," off *Zen Arcade* (SST, 1984)

13. Psychic TV, *Dreams Less Sweet* (Some Bizarre, 1983)

Chapter Seven
Come in Alone

"I would never deliberately dispel myths; they're generally much more interesting than reality."
　　　　　—Debbie Googe, in an email to the author

Loveless is largely recorded in mono. It took almost two years to record and turned hairs gray at the record label. It was made in so many different studios, it's nearly impossible to keep track. The only folks credited with production are Colm and Kevin. But a large number of engineers and assistants are listed: Alan Moulder, Anjali Dutt, Dick Meaney, Guy Fixsen, Darren Allison, Harold Burgon, Nick Robbins, Ingo Vauk, Nick Addison, Andy Wilkinson, Hugh Price, Charles Steel, Tony Falter, Adrian Bushby, Pascale Giovetto and Nick Savage.

　　Myths and half-truths abound. Some fans picture

Kevin working on the record nonstop, building up hundreds of layers of sound and erasing nearly all of them on a whim (the modern equivalent of self-styled "ethnopharmacologist" Harry Smith rolling the only copy of one of his handmade abstract films down the street in the rain, out of spite or craziness, or both). Detractors point to the many hours that Shields appeared to do nothing in the studio, and argue that without engineer Alan Moulder's helping hand, the record would have been a garbled mess.

After reading an earlier draft of this chapter, Kevin was upset. The book you are holding actually had to be pulled from the press. "You're referring to [*The Creation Records Story: My Magpie Eyes Are Hungry for the Prize* by David Cavanagh] too much," Kevin stated. "You know what happened to that book after it was released? It just died.So much of it was incorrect, and the weird thing is the whole thing was simply such a . . . bore. It's more an accountant's version of events, really. And as he hardly talked to anyone in the bands on Creation, there are so many great stories he missed," he says. "The guy who wrote it just disappeared after that book; you don't see [his byline] anywhere today. He was completely disgraced."

I can't back that up, nor do I care to. According to Shields, Cavanagh never spoke to anyone in MBV for his book. He contends the stuff on MBV in the book is "eighty percent made up." What's made up, exactly? It's basically axe-grinding by people who were barely involved in the record. "He did the natural thing, I guess, to call up everyone listed on the record, not realizing that most of the engineers did next to nothing," Shields says. What was printed seems to primarily be a weird excuse for engineers upset years later to just vent against the band. This seems really weird to me, 'cause if my name was on *Loveless* and I'd hardly done shit on the thing I'd try to hang my hat on it, if anything. Why knock the band?

Backstage on the *Loveless* tour in 1992, Colm swore up and down to me that a major reason the record had taken so long was because the band were having "chicken-eating contests, all the time" in the studio. (I didn't realize until much later that he was just taking the piss!) My favorite story comes via a friend of a buddy who worked on the sessions and, yes, wishes to remain anonymous. The dude swears that one day the engineers swapped Kevin's purple mic poppers (those round thin things that hang in the air in front of the mic, catching spit) with black ones. And allegedly he went ballistic, because he swore up and down that the purple ones sound much better.

In February of 1989, Alan McGee booked the band into Blackwing Recording Studios in Southwark. Shields explains that the group "went in there, and [McGee and Green] thought we could make another record in five days. But when it became clear that wasn't going to happen, they freaked out." Kevin dismisses the work done at Blackwing.

"The only notable part about what was recorded there is that we didn't release it." "Creation were never very supportive, but no one there did anything out of malice. And because we really were in our own world, it conspired to just be a dreadful experience. Alan McGee was obsessed with us sounding like *Isn't Anything*."

Shields explains that McGee spent "all of 1989" trying to get the band to release the *Isn't Anything* song "(When You Wake) You're Still in a Dream" as a single. "But we said no, we'd already gone beyond that song. Creation expected us to do things in a bizarrely short period of time, because that is how we'd worked before; they'd just lucked out with us in '88. These [Creation] guys were only 28 years old at the time, and taking lots of drugs. They were enthusiastic, but they really had no clue. We were pushing forward and they wanted us to release old stuff. The first sessions that were booked for *Loveless*, we had these few days in which we were expected to come up with a whole new album with an entirely new sound, which was much more studio-based. The work we did then was never unproductive—it was just moving towards something else. We went in, and ten days later we had four tracks recorded and mixed." "Moon Song," which was included on the *Tremolo* EP, came out of these sessions.

In September, MBV finally went back into a recording studio. McGee had chosen an inexpensive place for the band to work in, a basement studio called Elephant in

Wapping. The group spent eight weeks there. In-house engineer Nick Robbins complained to Cavanagh that Shields made it clear from the outset that he was not interested in hearing his opinions on anything, that he "was just there to press the buttons." Colm was homeless, sick and a wreck emotionally. The end result found him weakened; he couldn't use his legs properly so he couldn't lay the drum tracks down the way he and Kevin would have liked. The painstaking process of recording Colm so that his tracks could be sequenced began. Engineer Harold Burgon replaced Robbins. "He didn't do much, but he helped the group use the computer," Shields explains.

Over the course of recording *Loveless*, My Bloody Valentine were bounced around from cheap studio to cheap studio. Shields explains that the band listed every single person who was in the studio on the credits of the album because "even if all they did was fix tea," that might have had an effect on the album's outcome. This strikes me as a far more magnanimous approach than most artists take; can you imagine the Stones or Oasis doing that? Though clearly, the lack of any differentiation between roles on the record has opened the door for some engineers to claim more credit than they ever had. "What you have to realize is that these engineers—with the exception of Alan Moulder and later Anjali Dutt—were all just the people who came with the studio. And they were cheap studios to begin with. Everything we wanted to do was wrong according to them," he says.

"This guy Harold [Burgon], he was ranting and raving to us about his aesthetic of drum sounds and all that and when we it became clear we didn't care, we started arguing with him. He couldn't handle a band with their own opinions, their own idea of what they should sound like, basically. We had to put up with countless people like that. At that time, there weren't many people like me who didn't need engineers, who knew exactly what they wanted. This Nick Robbins guy, for instance—we recorded nothing while he was there; his sole contribution was tuning two of Colm's toms!"

McGee and Shields had agreed that before an album would be completed, the band would complete an EP, which would be called *Glider*. Shields and Burgon worked for three more weeks in another studio, Woodcray in Berkshire. "The people were all fucking idiots there," Shields sighs. "We did all the overdubs and feedback work there on [the song] 'Glider'; this is what got us dubbed completely mad!" Shields says. "People literally told me I was insane for doing that track. The engineers and owners of that studio treated us like shit; they poked fun of us to our face! So if we had an attitude towards engineers, well, that's why we had our attitude." Alan Moulder was brought in at Trident 2, a studio in Victoria, because the band had finished the song "Soon" and wanted him to mix it.

My Bloody Valentine then moved to Falconer, a studio in Chalk Farm, for mixing work, and again on to the Stone Room for more of the same. There were more studios on top of that, until the group settled for awhile at Falconer's other studio in Kentish Town. "We basically worked by ourselves at all these places, except for the mixing with Alan. As soon as we worked with him we realized we'd love to some more!"

That title track, "Glider," is a wordless, mildly discordant bombardment of looped, swirling and sampled basses and guitars dive-bombing each other. It just might be the most interesting thing the band ever did. When *Glider* was released, it hit the singles charts largely on the strength of the dance-pop hybrid track "Soon." No less an authority than Brian Eno was quoted as saying that song "set a new standard for pop. It's the vaguest music ever to have been a hit."

"I just wanted to mix my own album completely by myself," Shields says. "Just doing it by myself with an assistant from the studio coming in and operating the mixing desk when he had to. I liked working that way—it was more like a painter. It's like, if I want to paint a picture, I don't really need anybody to help me hold the brush or to suggest what colors I should use. And, I don't know much about the history of art, but what I do know is it's technology-based and like a new kind of blue would come in and be based on certain mixing techniques. So, a really good artist would need assistants to save him time by mixing paints. You need a trusted person who can actually do it. You can do it all yourself in theory but in energy and emotional energy you can't. That's the reality and that's why there are sixteen people on the credits to *Loveless*, even though Alan Moulder didn't actually do anything without my okay or my say-so."

"Of the sixteen people, only one of them did any EQ on any of the songs," Kevin says. "I trusted Moulder to put mics up on amps. He was so respectful; he was the only one I'd trust to do that. Even though I was controlling it, he knew what I wanted and we worked together. We never EQed anything on the album; it was always flat mic to tape even in the mixing. It's relatively untouched. All the other engineers credited either made tea or. . . . We had forty-five engineers but we said to them, 'We're so on this, you don't even have to come to work. If the boss says to come, you can but you're not coming into the studio. So they all just sat in the lobby. The sixteen guys credited just added a little positive input because I'm the one in control of the sound. We didn't need anyone; if there was a problem, I could solve it. People wouldn't understand me making Bilinda sing something over and over. I know just what I'm aiming for, and they just wouldn't understand it. So they would think I'm being really extreme and over the top, except for Moulder of course."

Alan Moulder had come on board "basically because he knew how to use an SSL desk," Kevin says. "We wanted to go to a good studio to mix it and it was an SSL studio. He was someone who worked with the Jesus and Mary Chain so we thought he would be really good to work with. And when we finished the *Glider* EP, we stopped working on the album and we actually went on a short tour to promote it. That added quite a few months as well because we were rehearsing, kind of getting our act together, and after the tour we sort of took our time going back into the studio. A lot of 1990 was kind of lost. Because we did this tour and then we started the record again probably in the spring, and then the summer was weird—I think it was the middle of the Gulf War. That was our great lost period, the summer of 1990. We probably spent three months working on constant feedback sampling and weird stuff where we were achieving something but, like expanding 'To Here Knows When' with loads and loads of weird stuff with drums and feedback. That would represent probably a three month period but we were really working slowly."

A second stop-gap EP, *Tremolo*, was recorded with Moulder. Later, all the bass tracks on *Loveless* were done with him in just five days. "Moulder was credited as an engineer, but he had a far greater role than that," Shields says. "He spiritually and emotionally supported us in a way that's not quantifiable. His belief in what we were doing helped keep us going big time. Having someone like him say 'This guy knows what he's talking about,' and 'Trust him' helped us a lot [with Creation]. That's why I mention him a lot. I try not to get people confused thinking that he was the producer, but he had a role to play that was far more than engineer. He was a true supporter, somebody I could really trust. Whenever he was around, I got way more work done, huge amounts of work in a small space of time. And then we'd go for months with hardly anything getting done." Moulder had to leave to go work on recordings for Shakespear's Sister, Ride and others. While he was gone, a young engineer named Anjali Dutt was brought in during the late spring of 1990. Together they recorded the vocal tracks for *Loveless* as well as a bit of guitar.

Asked to explain the overwhelming aspect of the album, Shields says, "You can make a record in certain ways that no matter what you played it on, it sounds kind of like the same balance, the same basic mix. I didn't want you to be able to get the vocals really loud if you play it one way, and too quiet another way. The relationship is the same, in the sense that you can't hear the vocals any clearer no matter which way you play them. They share too much of the same frequency as the guitar so you're giving the rhythm a lot of room to do that. If you have white noise, which is all frequencies at the same time, whatever you play it on it will be a different tone because what you're hearing is the tonality of the system. And pink noise is basically white noise with a frequency hump in it, like a bias of frequencies. And [*Loveless*] has more of a relationship to pink noise. The record isn't pink 'cause of that—but it's a weird coincidence."

"Basically the art of record making, in the classic sense, is to create something that sounds the same no matter where you hear it," Shields says. "Most people make records so that they sound the same everywhere. But to achieve that, you have to work with a limited frequency range. I wanted to make records that sound really different. Hearing it on a computer, the tiny little speakers off a computer, or hearing it played in a club, it's still basically what I wanted, which is that the guitar is fundamentally prominent. And that was very important, to always have the guitars louder than the vocals, no matter what. It's largely just the fact that the vocals have a place in the music, in a frequency sense, and they don't stick out more than some other sounds. *Loveless* was meant to sound really good if you play it loud on a ghetto blaster and also if you play it loud on a hi-fi. But you hear different things each way."

"When people make records, they have treble and basses for everything to kind of tame the mid-range and make it sweeter and more hi-fi sounding using stereo separation, reverb and ambience—to make everything sound big and spacious and wide," Kevin explains. "Everything I did is mostly mono: 'Soon' is mono, and 'To Here Knows When' is mono—there's no set area of separation. The sense of bigness just comes from the depth of perception. *Pet Sounds* and Phil Spector's productions were mono as well—it's more the balance of frequencies that creates a sense of depth than stereo separation and ambience; they're not as important. For me, everything that seemed to really affect me didn't affect me because I heard something coming out of one speaker and something else coming out of another speaker. The classic 80s version of stereo was basically a drum sound that's really widened by stereo effects and gated, and the guitars are really panned to extremes and it's just vocals and drums in the middle with overdubs. It was a corporate, weak sound."

For Shields, it was important to have a sound with "the guitar smack bang in the middle and no chorus, no modulation effect, which means that basically there are no chorus units, flangers, or phasers—no machines modulating the sound. I never used any of those except for one overdub on 'Blown a Wish.' There's a bit in that where you can hear this sort of wobbly guitar sound and that's this kind of thing called a Rotovibe pedal. And the one massive, big effect that we used a lot was a thing called reverse reverb, as well as reverse gated reverb. By having that effect on full and taking all the original guitar tone off, it allowed me to create this really ultra-melted guitar sound. That's the sound that's on 'To Here Knows When' and 'Blown a Wish.'"

What extent of the instruments did Shields play on *Loveless*? "I'm actually the only musician on the record except for the Colm song," Kevin says. "He did a song called 'Touched,' and that's all him." When asked what the recording process was like for her, Debbie recalls that is was "very strange really, because I had very little to do but wait—and it was a very long wait. At the beginning I used to go down most days but after a while I began to feel pretty superfluous so I went down less. I don't remember exactly how often I went in but by the end I think I was probably going in about half the time. It was weird though because although I didn't go in all the time I never went away. I kind of felt like I couldn't do anything else or go anywhere even though it was completely unnecessary for me to be there, so it was like being in limbo."

Chapter Eight
Swallow

Today it's taken for granted that indie musicians and fans are into (or at least respect) hip-hop and dance music—but way back in the 1980s that was far less common. In the UK of course, dance music was far less marginalized. But Kevin relates how "people had such a strong prejudice about rap music—and the Beastie Boys probably didn't help because of the gimmicky quality—but the fact of the matter is that people didn't know what they were hearing with rap. They just thought they were hearing 'ba ba ba ba da ba ba ba.' They didn't realize that there were infinite ways of doing it, all the weird ways of phrasing that are still changing and going on today. And for us it was 'Wow, this is very inspiring!' That was it in a nutshell; it was a big effect on things." In interviews from the late 80s, Shields often discussed his affinity for the Bomb Squad's production work on early Public Enemy recordings.

"We have a song called 'Slow' on the "You Made Me Realize" EP from '88 and if you listen to it, I'm not trying to rap or anything but it's influenced by [hip-hop]," he says. "The Mary Chain had done a song just before us like that called 'Sidewalking' where the vocal delivery was more percussive and more using kind of clichéd style phrasings and that was coming from hip-hop. It wasn't clichéd really it was just knowing the clichés, do you know what I mean? And the beat of that song—that was very hip-hop."

Upon its release, *Loveless* was picked apart by Simon Reynolds at *Melody Maker* for not being weirder or more electronic-sounding and danceable. In the *NME* review of the album, Dele Fadele wrote that "My Bloody Valentine have disassociated themselves from dance music and reggae bass lines, which will please some staunchly whitebread elements of their audience no end, but saddens me somewhat." Listening to the two pre-*Loveless* EPs again today, it's easy to see where people might have expected more songs like "Glider." Kevin says that "the big argument I was having with, especially a lot of student fanzine types during interviews on that tour, I kept going, 'I'm not trying to make a weird record; this isn't supposed to be weird—it's something organic.' That was my big catchphrase back then, 'organicness.'"

"I can make music that'd be properly weird, to the point of incomprehensibleness, but it doesn't have an emotional attachment," Shields says. "To me, when you have a person who's morphed into something that's not quite human it's far weirder than something that doesn't look vaguely recognizable. A strange jellyfish from under the ocean looks incredibly beautiful and totally alien, but doesn't freak people out as much as a human that's a little bit different looking. And that was the thing about *Loveless*; it's extreme simplicity and normalness mixed with just that feeling, an overall sense of this feeling. It was what it was, and the normalness—the simplicity—were key to that all being recognized."

The most radical changes in pop music occur with shifts that might appear really minor from the outside but actually represent huge leaps. Often, it's as simple as one tool being used for something it was never intended for, as with the turntable becoming a musical instrument via the scratch, or the 808 bass sampling keyboard getting tweaked to make crazy squelches. One of the things that flipped other musicians and producers out about *Loveless* is that the sampler is used as more than a phrase machine, largely because the band were sampling themselves.

"We chose organic sounds; that's why people didn't immediately go 'That's a keyboard,' even though it is. There are multilayered parts to some songs, like the opening of 'Only Shallow,' with me playing the same thing three or four times. It was the usual rock and roll bending the strings type of thing, but I had two amps facing each other, with two different tremolos on them. And I sampled it and put it an octave higher on the sampler. On *Glider*'s one guitar track, 'I Only Said,' that's one guitar track and a couple of overdubs. You can hear it has the movement of natural sound. The 'synth' solo two thirds of the way through 'Sometimes' is Bilinda's voice, and a little oboe sample in there from the keyboard itself."

"For us, where the sampler had a great value was that instead of having the option to play things on a keyboard based on some sounds you could find anywhere, we'd sample our own guitar feedback, which instead of just being one tone, it could be a tone having bends and quirks in it," Shields explains. "And then, by using the human voice as well for the top end, you've got these organic things happening, even though sometimes you're using keyboards to play them. You are letting the organic part be part of the rhythm of the sample. We'd edit them as such. God, so much of time we spent making the record was doing that kind of stuff. I mean, we did that massive experimentation thing in the summer of 1990, but before in 1989, one of the most sampled songs we created was 'Glider.' It's just a guitar riff, and then something that sounds like gates creaking— and that's all guitar feedback, loads and loads of guitar feedback that we just sampled and played in. But in those days we didn't have a keyboard so we played it all by pressing the button on the sampler. So there wasn't even a keyboard involved. It was just touching the sample itself you know?"

"Most of the songs have got samples on them," Kevin says. "On 'Soon,' there's a bit that goes 'ah ah ah' where it sounds like Belinda's voice—that's just me hitting a key on the sampler—well it was actually a Bell delay unit, but we made a sample out of it. And the first thing in 'Only Shallow'—those kind of high sounds—that's just a sample." At the time, they were fumbling in the dark to use these methods, but Shields notes that "everything we did is just now stock, normal, standard techniques for making music. We were just using the technology to achieve our aims." Everyone else at the time using samplers, like Pop Will Eat Itself or Age of Chance, "used their technology to make it sound like technology (stutters intentionally)—that 'N-N-N-N-Nineteen' type thing. What we did—and which then became the prominent way of using samplers—was to try and make it sound like you're *not* using a sampler."

Chapter Nine
To Here Knows When

After *Glider*, time was spent in even more studios, often for just a day. Finally, Kevin settled (primarily) on a place called Protocol in Holloway, and work began in earnest in May of 1990 on another EP, as well as tracks for *Loveless* proper (one track from each EP wound up on the album). "I got involved just after the *Glider* EP was done," Guy Fixsen recalls. Fixsen was chief engineer at Protocol at the time; MBV brought along Anjali with them, and later Moulder. "I did a lot of work on the *Tremolo* EP. I spent my twenty-second birthday recording the tambourine for that song. Can't think of any way I would rather have spent it! And actually the following five days—that's right, a whole week just on a tambourine part! But in all I spent about eighteen months of my life working on *Loveless*, which, as far as I know, is longer than any other engineer worked on it. It was a bizarre and inspiring way to spend eighteen months, that's for sure. There were a few gaps for various reasons—mostly me doing some of my first productions such as Moonshake, Moose, the Telescopes, or the band being elsewhere to mix and so on."

The folks at Creation thought at first that the song "To Here Knows When," with its elastic and intentionally warped sounds, might have been recorded onto a faulty tape or something. They were not as enthusiastic about this release, which came out in February of 1991. But to fans, both EPs clearly showed that *Loveless* was going to be worth waiting for, assuming it ever got finished anyway. *Tremolo* reached number twenty-nine in the charts, their first time in the top thirty. "The EPs are their own thing, in a weird kind of way, 'cause they are rougher," Kevin says. "There's a different mood to them."

Moulder returned to the sessions in August and was surprised by how little work had been completed, according to Cavanagh's book. Shields continued to try his luck at other studios, and kept encountering faulty equipment and the like. McGee and Green were starting to freak out over the cost of the album. Deb relates how the tension between the label and the band "was definitely something that Kevin was much more aware of; he was the only one that really talked to Alan on the phone. However, I probably went into the office more than the others, because I lived near the office at the time. And also because I was often the only one awake during the day (as I hadn't been at the studio all night). I went with Ann Marie (Kevin's sister and the band's manager) quite a few times for various reasons during the recording of the album and it was completely obvious towards the end that they had really lost patience." Moulder left again in March, for good this time, to work with the Jesus and Mary Chain.

"It was bizarre how many little technical glitches, computer huffs and extraneous noises made their way into the process," Fixsen says. "Partly it was Kevin's all-seeing quality control that sounded the alarm at problems that a lot of people would miss entirely. Partly it was the amount of time spent that pushed the improbability envelope. Partly it was just plain spooky!" From Fixsen's perspective, the reason it took so long is due to "Kevin's high level of quality control set against the low level of quality control in a lot of the places the record was recorded in, but also because of the pressure the band was under from listeners and business people, and at times some bizarre technical problems. It was also down to the high level of creative ambition. It does take time to genuinely experiment without missing the point."

"I wasn't party to that many conversations between them and when I was it just seemed to be pretty normal 'How's it coming along guys?' sort of stuff," Fixsen says. "As Alan McGee said to me and Colm at one point, he had plenty of other bands spending his money at a far more furious rate than the Valentines. He said they were a cheap date in comparison. That was half the problem really; they were doing battle with an array of cheap studios and the problems inherent in that, but at least they were relatively cheap. The pace of the record started pretty good but as things get more protracted in any recording project, motivation is harder to come by and things slowed down progressively. After having dealt with all sorts of technical nonsense at a whole bunch of studios, which really does sap your energy, Kevin needed things to be 'just so' to be able to get his teeth into exploring an idea. Having said that, we sure watched a lot of TV! There was a point where Alan came into the studio and told Kevin that Creation might well go under and the pace quickened a bit after that."

Several more studios were used for vocals and, finally, the record was mixed with Dick Meaney at the Church in Crouch End. When asked if she ever thought, "OK, this really is taking too long," Deb replies, "I'm sure I did, but to be honest time becomes pretty abstract when something goes on that long; part of me thought it would never finish. When it was actually finished, that was really shocking."

To what extent *Loveless* really came close to bankrupting Creation is debatable. Dick Green is alleged to have begged McGee to pull the plug on the project entirely, twice. McGee says the only way in the end that he could fund the album was to borrow money from his pops, something he said he'd never do. Pat Fish aka Creation recording artist the Jazz Butcher lamented in *Magpie Eyes* to Cavanagh that "no one could afford to eat because of Kevin Shields." Green's hair turned gray by the time the album came out, and he was just thirty. It was blamed on *Loveless*. Vinita Joshi, who runs Rocket Girl records in London and now functions as Kevin's manager, reflects that "it's probably something that got blown out of proportion and the comment stuck. If a record label has several artists each recording an album, and there are no significant releases during that time, then there is going to be a cash flow problem. It's a regular occurrence with independent labels, but I think it is unfair to aim that at one band."

"At the onset of *Loveless*, a mutual plan was drawn out between the two parties, or Alan and Kevin, with Dick as the moderator, who made weekly checks on the band's progress," Ed Ball explains. "But as the plan kept being constantly remodified, it ended with Creation variously trying to cajole, demand and blackmail an album out of the Valentines. In the end, it came down to protracted birth thing with Alan as the very hands-on midwife to this extraordinary beast. Every day there would be an air that this could be the last week of the label-scary but strangely exciting to be in that situation. It was a very real situation. I do remember discussing with Alan my theory that some of the titles of Valentine songs were signposted to him-I now call this the MBV code."

"I have since raised this with Kevin and he says there's

nothing in it, but please indulge me; its most entertaining," Ball says. "1) After months and months and months chasing Kevin for a single, only to be greeted with 'Yeah, soon,' Alan finally gets the track as the first single from the project called . . . 'Soon.' 2) After months and months and months chasing Kevin for listening copies of anything recorded to hear, Alan is appeased with another single called 'To Here Knows When.' 3) After months and months and months of chasing and haranguing and a relationship in tatters, verging on hate, the album is delivered, packaged and called . . . *Loveless*. And it doesn't end there: 4) When the Valentines signed to Island, the only recording they got off the band was a cover version of Louis Armstrong's 'We've Got All the Time in the World.' I'm very proud of this theory and I really do believe that it was Kevin's subconscious at work."

Without a doubt, Shields was under a lot of stress. Imagine being in a studio for hours on end, for months on end, some of it with your girlfriend and artistic collaborator, with whom you are not getting along at the time and you totally love her. That alone is stressful enough, right? But wait—you also are afraid that your girl's highly unstable and potentially violent ex might show up at any minute. And your record label seems about to pull the plug at any moment, and you feel they never supported you properly anyway, and you can't remember the last full night's sleep you had, and everyone is calling you a goddamn genius or the new Brian Wilson which means what, that they expect you to be playing in a sandbox any day now? Everyone is wondering when your new record is going to come out, and the kid bands down the street are copping what you did last year—only with like no finesse at all if we're gonna be honest about it—they're making a ton of dough while you don't know how you're going to pay the rent. And this record, it was supposed to be done many months ago but everything that could go wrong has—including maybe there are, like, ghosts in the studio or something? And one of your best friends, your drummer, is really sick and can't even play. I mean, what the fuck?

"It was an unfortunate time for us domestically," Kevin explains. "And going to the studio was a way of getting away from the shit that we were in. It was just unfortunate you know, trying to make a record that's actually a good record when you've got nothing else going for you. There was also crazy stuff with Bilinda, as at the time her ex was threatening violence to her, and threatening to kidnap her son, and it sort of led to me having to answer the door with a hammer in my hand, for a long time. We used a lot of the time in the studio to just eat and relax and then we'd just do maybe, it probably averaged out a couple of hours a day. For me, part of the process is being in the studio and then allowing that creative energy that occurs from the excitement of starting a record to be a real catalyst for those new songs. In that first four to eight week period, I had another room where I would write and the studio found out and were like, 'What are you doing?' Nowadays a lot of what we did is normal, but back then it was just seen as wrong—'You're not rich rock stars; you can't come in here and sit down with some guitar in another room and write songs!'"

"Also, our own context was that we had turned down big record deals with majors," Kevin says. "We could have had proper lifestyles but in order to stay independent and fully in control we were broke. So our attitude was that while Creation can't give us anything but studio time, we're going to use that time to get our act together and make a good record. We didn't feel guilty. We were like, 'It will be all right in the end and it's just the way it is.' One thing that you should be aware of is just what the whole thing about us spending 250 thousand pounds and Creation nearly going bankrupt is definitely a myth. Alan McGee thought it would be cool. He always exaggerates anyway and he always said it will do you more good than harm. If you look in to a rock encyclopedia it'll mention our name and all they'll say is, 'The band who spent loads of money and nearly bankrupted Creation.' That'll sometimes be the only thing they'll say. The basic facts were that Creation left Rough Trade distribution. We started the record with Creation literally being penniless. They weren't bankrupt, because they didn't in fact owe anything. When we finished the record we were no longer homeless and they had like ten bands, with half of them getting into the charts. They were an extremely healthy label. That's the actual truth."

"The amount we spent nobody knows because we never counted. But we worked it out ourselves just by working out how much the studios cost and how much all the engineers cost," Shields explains. "160 thousand pounds was the most we could come to as the actual money that was spent. The only thing that ever does annoy me when *people* talk about us spending Creation's money is that when we started *Loveless*, we had started a licensing deal with Warner Brothers which was going to give much needed cash to the project and basically they advanced 70 thousand dollars that was then worth probably about 50 or 40 thousand pounds. Between that money and the fact that *Isn't Anything* we made very cheaply . . . that was selling really well at the time, and the two EPs were selling really well. By the time we finished *Loveless*, with the EPs and the first Creation album, we probably sold a couple hundred thousand records."

"Creation never showed us any accounts, even to this day," Shields laments. "It's important for people to understand that when we worked out how much we'd spent, we realized that it was almost all our own money. Because the first record and EPs had been made for so little money, Creation probably spent fifteen to twenty thousand pounds of their own money on it, and that's it. They never showed us any accounts, and then they got bought out by Sony."

"Over the years, it just became this myth that was like, yeah, you know, it got to the point where Creation spent half a million dollars or pounds and they never recouped the money and they nearly went bankrupt and they had to sell to Sony and it was only Oasis who saved them. And the message being put across is that art isn't worth it if it's not financially viable, no matter how good it is. Part of the critical value of the thing is its financial worth in the corporate world. It's weird. That change happened particularly in the 90s; it was solidified then. Instead of the record company being the bad guys it's the band, the creative people are the bad guys taking poor corporate company's money, oh how terrible. And it's fucked, you know what I mean?"

After everything, Ball felt that *Loveless* was a huge artistic triumph. "This record made by Kevin under extreme artistic circumstances, midwifed by Alan, this unloved monster destroyed everything held dear by Radio One producers and the Engineers Guild, making a mockery of Rock Stereo Orientation. The two singles were to the 90s what 'Strawberry Fields Forever' and 'I Am the Walrus' were to the 60s, 'Anarchy in the UK' and 'God Save the Queen' were to the 70s, 'Love Will Tear Us Apart' to the 80s—or something." But reached via email, Alan McGee clearly has no interest in rehashing the story of *Loveless*. "Sorry; that record fucking bores me," he replies, adding "Long live the Libertines, Dirty Pretty Things and Babyshambles."

Chapter Ten
Forever and Again

Drummer Colm O'Ciosoig is the phantom of *Loveless*. Most of the percussion tracks on the album were painstakingly programmed from samples. It's like he's there, but he's not really there. Sure, he contributed the awesome, minute-long, ambient "mating whales" track, "Touched." But mostly, he's there as an electronic ghost; like a Xerox stuck into a painting, the way Basquiat used to throw color Xeroxes of his own drawings made at Ed's Copy Shop onto his canvases, and then paint on top of them.

Colm's absence is really weird, as live, and on their previous recordings, Colm is MBV's secret weapon. He had to be one of the only drummers in the world loud enough to compete with the rest of the band's wall of squall. Check his drumming on *Isn't Anything*. He's really *on* like a metronome, but he throws these little, melodic, jazzy accents all over the place. "Emptiness Inside": it's Steve Shelley on steroids! Those fills on "You Never Should" are almost off, but they're perfect. "Feed Me With Your Kiss" is Keith Moon after taking lessons from Milford Graves; it's sick.

Speaking of sick, that's what Colm was for much of the recording of *Loveless*, which was a long-ass time obviously, and that's why so much of the recording happened without him. "He had a really hard time when we were doing the record," Bilinda relates. "It's such a shame, 'cause he's such a brilliant drummer. He just wasn't at his best at all. I think it all just really took its toll on him, having trouble with just about everything in his personal life: nowhere to live, and his girlfriend had to go back to America—she was going through some hard times herself and stuff—and he just couldn't function the way he normally would. He just couldn't drum the way he normally would. The drums ended up being compromised because of that; Kevin's not a drummer. He's got a good sense of rhythm, but he couldn't just take over for him and do his job, so a lot of that [translated to] more programming than was anticipated, which caused a lot of stress." Later, when the band toured the songs, "He actually learned all the stuff after not having done it; it was a sort of different process, you know."

"With the arrangements—it's exactly what Colm would have done, it just took much longer to do." Shields stresses that the drums sound exactly the way they would have if Colm had played them all live. "Colm only played proper drums on two tracks," Shields says. "The song 'Only Shallow' has Colm playing live drums, 'cause he'd gotten better then." Shields brings at least part of O'Ciosoig's predicament to bear on the record label. "We were in the studio and didn't have any equipment. We were promised two grand by Creation and we never got it. It was a cold autumn; we were both homeless and had been squatting, which gave us a better lifestyle than being in some crummy flat. So we did a deal with Creation. We were on the dole for 50 pounds a week and once we were paid 70 pounds by Creation, which doesn't pay for rent and living, we lost the dole money and had to apply for income-based assistance. It's all complicated and harder to get a place to live than even if you're on the dole, because you're on a ridiculously low income. Colm and his girlfriend got thrown out of the place they were living in and Creation were completely broke at the time. They'd just left Rough Trade distribution and were penniless and literally couldn't afford like 100 pounds."

"So they stuck us in the studio and hoped for the best, which wasn't really working out because Colm needed somewhere to live and he needed 300 pounds for a deposit," Kevin says. "Creation just wouldn't give it to him; they just told him to fuck off and not to even ask for money. It all became too much for him. He hadn't anywhere to live and couldn't find another squat. They were telling him to look for a squat after recording, which would be like one in the morning. Then he got really bad flu mixed with all that stress. His girlfriend was being deported. She was from America and caught working in an after hours bar. It all got too much and he just lost it. He couldn't even use his legs! That's why he ended up not being involved in the normal way."

"We would be trying to do these tracks and Colm wouldn't be able to; we tried to program the bass pedal because he couldn't use his legs any more and he wanted to play live over the top," Shields says. A slew of drum tracks were recorded this way, but when time came to play guitar over the top, "it was like playing along to a human and a machine with no groove to it, and we realized it was a waste of time. So we had to program all the stuff he was playing. We sampled his sounds, not trying to have them sound like a machine, [although] his parts were quite like that anyway. It wasn't a terrible tragedy; it was more like, 'This is a fuck up but we're gonna get there any way.' We didn't know how to work the machines and didn't have anyone there to do it for us—we were totally out there in the wilderness. But we managed to do it with people who had little roles, like Harold Burgon helped with the operating of the computer."

Oh, wait. Maybe I should have called Debbie "the phantom of *Loveless*"? After all, she doesn't play a note on the record, even though she's listed as "bass" in the credits. When asked if she felt left out, Deb replies "Yes, definitely. On the one hand I completely understood Kevin's motives. I mean you wouldn't expect a painter to feel happy about other people coming in and putting their little marks all over their painting. *Loveless* was very much Kevin's thing; it was impossible to know what was going on his head. Even if I had played the bass lines he'd made up, I wouldn't have had the same feel or touch as Kevin and that would have bothered him, which I completely appreciate. But it's not nice to feel totally superfluous. And I think the knock-on effect of that was that I didn't go in as much as the others and that resulted in me feeling like a bit of an outsider at times, plus of course Kevin and Colm had known each other forever and Kevin and Bilinda were living together. That added to that feeling of alienation at times."

Bilinda confirms that Debbie isn't on the record, and adds that "the guitar parts that I would play live, Kevin basically did all of it on the record," too. I wondered if that was ever tough on her ego or anything. Bilinda answers that she "was never a great guitarist, and for Debbie—for Kevin to actually translate to Debbie what he had in his head and play it right would have been an agonizing process. I think Debbie, because she later went off and did her own music, would have liked to do that. And the whole thing with the band deteriorating when we had the studio later, maybe there were issues with people wanting to do more, but it's not like there wasn't room for someone to make up a song. I think Kevin would have welcomed that, and I know he was really pleased to have Colm's piece included."

"The really important thing about Colm's drumming on the record is that the drums sound exactly how they were supposed to sound," Kevin stresses. "Of course there's the exception of songs where we wanted it to sound sampled, like on 'Soon,' the parts were supposed to sound like that. Otherwise, people can't tell the difference between Colm's playing and his not playing, when it had been sampled and sequenced. We worked very hard to make it relatively seamless. I've had people in the studio, playing them the master tapes, and asked them if they could tell which tracks had live drums and which didn't, and they couldn't tell the difference. We had lost the Who-type influence and were going for something more simplistic, more pure. And with Bilinda and Debbie—you have to remember that they really just weren't there for so much of the recording, especially Debbie. She was never there."

Chapter Eleven
I Only Said

"Sometimes when I want to write lyrics, I'll listen to *Loveless*. Because of the way the vocals are buried, you can almost listen to the songs as if they're instrumental pieces."
—Bob Pollard of Guided by Voices, interviewed by the author in 2001

Part an abstraction of 60s backing vocals and partly a whole-sale improvement on the Cocteau Twins' moaning croons, MBV's breathy vocal style is unique and lovely. It's also impossible to describe without using the word "ethereal." That's partly due to the low volume they're usually at in the overall mix, but also the lovely high pitch that Kevin and Bilinda often sang in. Bilinda disallows that there's much special about her vocal style, arguing that she was just copying the way that Kevin used to sing back up for Dave.

"Because it took so long to do the vocals, and because the melodies were in my head since '89 and we didn't do them until '91, I couldn't tolerate really clear vocals, where you just hear one voice," Kevin explains. "I'd heard it indistinctly in the studio for so many years (with scratch vocals on the tracks) that it had to be more like a *sound*. So that's why, when we'd had all the vocals, what was slightly eccentric about it, slightly only, was that we had so many vocals on one reel. We had a separate twenty-four track reel with between ten and seventeen vocal tracks on there. And because they couldn't really face analyzing them, I realized just by a wonderful coincidence that Bilinda and I have a tendency to sing things really similarly each time. So it was easy just to bring all the vocals up, eliminating the ones that weren't good all the way through. And what you hear there is all the ones that are left. And then we'd just take one, one that I particularly like, and ever so slightly edge it forward, so that the articulation's coming more from that. But then the sound and the whole thickness of it's coming from ten or fifteen vocals on each track." If you'll allow me to be a master of the obvious, the way the vocals are recorded, with shit-loads of layers, is not how the guitars were done, even though it's how most folks assume the guitars were done! Meanwhile, the Internet legend about the vocals has them being recorded in one take while half-asleep.

The indecipherability of MBV's lyrics is deliberate, and is a key element of their sound. Lyrics aren't printed anywhere on the band's albums, except in Japan where lyrics have to be printed out, and those are hilariously inaccurate. The only way I know any MBV lyrics at all is by rewinding tracks obsessively, or trolling obsessive fan sites to see whose take on the tunes seems most likely. Kevin laughs when I ask him if any of these are correct. "They're all wrong," he says gleefully. "It bothers me only in the sense that all of the lyrics are much more stupid and pretentious and flowery than what we wrote. On our website for a laugh I was thinking we would rate these sites on a percentage of rightness. Instead of saying which lyrics are right or wrong we'll say, 'This site is 90 percent wrong,' or, 'This site is 75 percent wrong.'"

"How all the lyrics come about is that when I make up a tune I just sing whatever and I realize that there's actually most of the song there when you listen to it," Kevin says. "I'm singing stuff unconsciously, and then if it does make sense but it's not proper grammar, and I like the way it sounds, I'll just leave it. People will be going, 'I can't work the lyrics out,' but if I were actually to tell you word for word what they are, you would say, 'Of course I can hear that, it's totally clear.' The sentences are broken so a line will finish like halfway through and then the next bit will come afterwards. If you were to see it on a piece of paper it does actually make sense."

When I was eight or nine and first started to become a music freak, I was really drawn to pop and rock songs that were scary and indecipherable. Glossalalic, obscure lyrics shouted, chanted and sung atop music that implies volume—I dug that shit a lot. There are songs that scar you for life because they just sounded so big and heavy and impenetrable (that's the kind of babble Patti Smith was going on about in *Babel*, no?) at one point. Later, they usually sound ridiculous. There was a hit song in 1977 called "Black Betty" by Ram Jam, basically a cocaine unicorn proto-rap delivered by sleazy Southern rockers. To my young ears, though, the speed of the lyrical delivery sounded alien and really cool. It took me many listens to decipher the words. I think I liked the song best before I understood it. It was a puzzle; don't all kids love puzzles?

Lyrics are one area where Shields was more open to input from others. Bilinda wrote about a third of the lyrics on *Isn't Anything* and *Loveless*. Most rock lyrics are ridiculous, even before you cut and paste them out of one of those websites that shoots twenty-two pop-ups at your face to try and see what the words to "Popozao" are. Not enough rock music has words that you simply cannot understand. "Wolves, Lower" by R.E.M., "Pay to Cum" by the Bad Brains, "Madame George" by Van Morrison—part of what makes these songs such total classics is that no matter how many times you listen, you never really know the words.

"Words are extremely important in the sense that we've spent way more time on the lyrics than ever on the music,"

Shields says. "Music is spontaneous and it's either good or bad so you just take it or leave it. Where lyrics, all the stuff comes out and then we usually just finish them right before we have to sing so it's usually these nights of eight or ten hours just trying to desperately make sure it's going to be as good as possible, even though most of it's there anyway and it's always been there. There's nothing worse than bad lyrics. For me a bad lyric is a lyric that jumps out at you, and that's offensive, it takes you completely away from enjoying the music." Amen to that.

Chapter Twelve
When You Wake
You're Still in a Dream

ME: You spoke with Kevin about the sleep deprivation thing going on?

GUY FIXSEN: I'm not sure what this is about; I know he often had problems sleeping though.

I've always been attracted to songs about being dizzy, confused and/or lost in dreams—"Circles (Instant Party)" by the Who, "Dizzy" by Tommy Roe, "Mixed-Up Confusion" by Jimi Hendrix, "The Sound of Confusion" by Spacemen Three, "I Dreamed I Dream" by Sonic Youth, "Dream Baby Dream" by Suicide—absolute favorites, all of them. I especially dig the way these tunes use certain structural elements to reinforce the lyrical content, generally employing exaggeratedly woozy and/or nursery rhyme-ishly swoopy sounds to mimic a loss of control.

MBV's sound is so clearly bent and disorientating, as are what lyrics one may easily discern, and several of the band's tunes deal with dreams: "(You're) Safe in Your Sleep (From This Girl)," "(When You Wake) You're Still in a Dream" and "When You Sleep." It's no surprise that *Loveless* is often associated with altered states of consciousness, whether through dreams, sex, the state of being in love or drugs. It's often assumed that MBV were total drug fiends but not so, according to Bilinda. "Kevin and Colm took ecstasy but not a lot," she says. "I tried it and didn't like it, you know, palpitations and stuff. Kevin, the whole time he was with Alan McGee, and Colm, they were pretty into it, you know. And later hanging around with Primal Scream there was a bit of coke going around, and parties. We never got into it really, but Colm did a bit. But doing *Loveless*, the only bit of relaxation afterwards was before we went to bed, you know. Later, [the pot use] really accelerated when we moved to the house in Streatham."

But Shields' favorite method of achieving altered states was not such a rock star cliché as drugs. Especially while recording an album, he would not sleep much at all during the process, and would record late at night as well, at times achieving what's called a hypnagogic state. Andreas Mavromatis' *Hypnagogia: The Unique State of Consciousness Between Wakefulness and Sleep* roughly defines hypnagogic experiences as "hallucinatory and quasi-hallucinatory events taking place in the intermediate state between wakefulness and sleep."

"The *Isn't Anything* phase was big time about sleep deprivation," Kevin says. "I was young enough and strong enough and not into drugs enough. I wasn't smoking lots of dope or anything, because if you smoke enough pot you can't stay awake. I would get off on just having two or three hours of sleep a night and work constantly and it was very enjoyable. For *Loveless*, I had become more immersed in a general state of slight dislocatedness. You see, there's a subconscious kind of way of using language that's more impressionistic than the normal way. The way that people speak in their sleep—people are slightly incoherent but it's not less real. The structure isn't as formed and as focused. It was just a case of having all of our unconscious stuff and just honing it into something that was acceptable. That was a big part of my life for a long time."

While recording *Isn't Anything*, Shields was "in an extreme lack of sleep state" at the studio in Wales. "And it was out there, that's the only way I can describe it. I was having experiences like real classic stuff from cheap UFO movies. I'd be by myself in the studio, which was a barn away from where everyone else was staying, and there in the middle of nowhere in this barn trying to write lyrics, and one night I couldn't stay awake but I had to finish the lyrics, and then, while falling asleep, I heard this huge roaring noise. And the room was all bright and I was crawling across the floor, desperately crawling under the desk trying to stay awake long enough to finish these lyrics, while feeling completely surrounded by the presence of things."

"We found out later that the whole place is supposed to be haunted, and all sorts of weird things had happened" Kevin says. "The engineer wasn't telling us that it was haunted. That's part of the policy of the studio, that you don't tell the clients it's haunted because they start getting freaked out, because weird things happen and because it's in the middle of nowhere and all that shit. And, also it's near the military base, so there were weird planes flying above all the time and pulling sonic booms. My whole memory of making that record was just this constant sense of presence, like it was a mixture of angels and, funnily enough, cow ghosts, ghosts of cows. I don't know why, but I kept having this impression of bloody animals and cows all the time—really big, weird faces with big brown eyes. But not like aliens."

"By and large most of the lyrics come from, not so much the hypnagogic half-awake half-asleep state, but more the slightly trancey state that you're in when you're writing songs," he (sort of) explains. "And that does involve being quite tired. Most tunes I write it's really late at night, or if it's in the studio it's after a few weeks of being in the studio not really getting good sleep. And being in a room full of electronic equipment I find quite mind altering as well, somehow. I don't know why, but I feel very affected by a lot of electricity. And that's why for me the record making process involves a lot of getting away from the studio. Being in there for a long time it's kind of like, I'm going off; I'm losing reality, day by day, slightly. Do you know what I mean?"

Of course, similar experiments were conducted by such spiritual-minded aesthetes as the Surrealist-associated *Grand Jeu* group headed by Rene Daumal in the 30s. Kevin isn't familiar with them in particular, and claims to only have glanced through one book on Surrealism, but he obviously took away a lot from it. "Surrealism wasn't coming from a social perspective, by taking social things and making juxtapositions of them," he says. "It was coming from inner information, it was coming from in the inner worlds, those combinations of imagery and situations are natural. They weren't superficial; it was deep, and that's why it has a deep resonance."

I ask Kevin if he's aware of the Dream Machine experiments that Brion Gysin and William S. Burroughs got into in the 60s. "Actually, that's funny," he says. "I was thinking about that the other day, because we played this gig with Primal Scream in France, at a festival in Rennes. The guy who does our lights has the tendency to make the strobes really extreme sometimes. I closed my eyes, and whatever frequency it was, I suddenly was totally tripping, and I was going into inner space, right there on stage, and it was really cool, and then he stopped the light and it was just that particular frequency. Usually it's just, you know, the strobe effect where you see stuff in front of your eyes when you close them and it's really interesting. But this time it immediately kicked in to encourage the theta brainwaves. It's probably about time that I found out what those frequencies are and do something with that, just for the hell of it."

There are kits on the Internet where you can assemble your own Dream Machine, though if you want to really trip out from simply watching the alternation of bright light, take any chance you ever get to see Tony Conrad's *The Flicker* projected in a theatre (assuming you do not have a heart condition or suffer from seizures). For the post-*Loveless* tour, the band wanted some sort of visual element that matched the music, but they'd stopped receiving any funding from Creation and were broke. Thankfully, Angus Cameron, the guy who shot the cover and videos for the album, had a series of short abstract loops that the group were able to pick up on the cheap. "It was quite haphazard in a way," says Shields, "the way it came together, but [it worked]. The statement for the tour was primarily the energy, using the force of volume to make audiences pay attention whether they wanted to or not. And it was the same with the visuals, which force people to pay attention, but not really. You know [with the abstract looping] it was a constant sameness in a way, like a modern version of the psychedelic thing in a way. But rather than trying to imitate the effects of acid, we were more trying to induce it, you know what I mean?"

Chapter Thirteen
Honey Power

Taking a break from work, I drop by to visit Kami and April, two thirty-something music fiends who dance at Magic Gardens, a small strip club located in a section of downtown Portland that used to be a funky, excellent Chinatown and is now getting a "facelift" to make it more tourist-friendly. And despite its low-key, neighborhood bar type vibe, Magic Gardens is generally considered to be the best club in a town with more strip clubs per capita than any other in the US. The place is frequented by rock stars, who drop by late at night while road crews pack up their gear. The song "Sometimes" comes on and, ever the egoist, I ask Kami if the tune is being played for me, since I've told her a dozen times I'm writing a book about this record. "It's a mistake," she replies, laughing at me a little bit. "But I can't dance to this shit!," she adds. This surprises me; women at this place dance to stuff you'd never expect anyone to: Iron and Wine, Patsy Cline, Can, Ween, Dungen, Soft Cell, Suicide, even the Sun City Girls. But never "Girls, Girls, Girls."

"It's just too . . . emotional," she explains, about the song. Then Kami rolls her eyes, shrugs and moves very slowly and gracefully across the small, low stage as the song plays. Swathed in red light, she watches with seeming disinterest as bills make their way to the edge of the "rack." This is not the kind of place where people stuff bills into g-strings; people keep their distance. Kami's little dance to "Sometimes" is lovely, despite her reservations about it. I wish I could show it to you, but we're not in that part of the future where books have Quicktime videos imbedded in them, so you'll just have to use your imagination.

What Kami said really got me thinking, though. Just a record or so earlier, MBV had songs with titles such as "Soft as Snow (But Warm Inside)" and lyrics that went, for instance, "Get in your car and drive it all over me" or, "Kiss kiss kiss uh suck suck suck." Bilinda had written a third of the songs on *Isn't Anything*, including the crowd pleasing "Several Girls Galore." "Cupid Come" has the lines "Swallow me into your bed / With glimpses of your thighs / Forget your vanity / Come cupid come," or I think that's what they are. But they're more abstract on *Loveless*, the song titles less sexualized. It's still a very sexy record, it's just more complicated. On the first song, "Only

Shallow," Bilinda sings, "Soft as a pillow touch her there / Where she won't dare, somewhere" in her most ultimately sexy voice. The backing guitar line sounds like a mechanical beast gone crazy. As Heather Phares puts it in All Music Guide: "*Loveless* intimates sensuality and sexuality instead of stating them explicitly; Kevin Shields and Bilinda Butcher's vocals meld perfectly with the trippy sonics around them, suggesting druggy sex or sexy drugs."

The sexuality may be charged, but it's ambiguous. James Hunter, writing in the *SPIN Alternative Record Guide*, assumes that the two high-pitched vocalists on *Loveless* are Debbie and Bilinda, when in fact of course it's Kevin and Bilinda: "The women manage great feats because, even when their singing lies several layers beneath the foregrounded accompaniments, the sweet timbres of their voices alternately sting, caress or upbraid." In his Amazon.com review of the album, Douglas Wolk plays up the record's sexual angle, calling it a "pure, warm, androgynous but deeply sexual rush of sound" that is "furiously loud but seductive rather than aggressive . . . pulsing like a lover's body." Bilinda occasionally sang the lower register and Kevin the higher one. I love that, and ask Kevin about it. "Yeah that's the thing; Bilinda always had a very girly voice, but also a bit low," he says. "I had a slight androgynous edge to myself I suppose," Shields continues. "When I was younger, I was half-influenced by female singers as I was by male singers. Sometimes when I'd be having trouble singing a song, I'd just have to think of Dusty Springfield or something. And that sounds mad, but that would really help. And Björk; she would be a bit of an influence just because of her fearlessness."

MBV's very composition appeals in its sexual symmetry: straight dude, gay woman, discreet couple. Sounds like the start of a "casual encounters" post on Craigslist. Speaking of ads, they were no Benetton commercial, but there was a diversity to their sizes: Colm all small and wiry like a soccer forward; Kevin big and strong, a bit of extra weight on his frame but cute with his long hair; Deb all curvy and slightly butch in her shortish hair and penchant for trousers; and then Bilinda with her slight, model-type looks and huge eyes that look straight out of a Margaret Keane painting. The boy-girl-boy-girl make up of the group was really important to Shields. "Yes—it was a balance of energy! Even on tour, we tried to balance the crew. We desperately didn't want a bunch of rock and roll crew people." Along with Kevin's sister Ann-Marie, "We'd have various other girls on tour, like, selling t-shirts, and it kept it good. The female energy is so powerful, and I need that around me, to this day. Even when I'm thinking about doing my own solo stuff, although the first thing I do will be my own thing, I know it will morph into a band with girls in it. I know it will."

Chapter Fourteen
No More Sorry

Everything about this album feels so oblique, so gauzy and hazy and inscrutable, that I never realized the album's title was actually straightforward, almost literal. Then I spoke with Kevin and Bilinda for this book, and it seemed apparent that the title referred directly to the disintegration of their relationship, which was happening right then and there, in the studio. It was happening even more slowly than the recording process itself, but it was happening. (I know I keep inserting myself into the narrative here, but I hope I'm not painting myself as some great close friend with insider knowledge. Yeah, they almost gave me a song for free once, and we had a few pals in common, whoop dee doo. Besides, the few times I was backstage, I was so awestruck by Bilinda and Debbie that I never spoke with them. They were both so rad and beautiful, and at the time,

I barely knew how to talk to women at all let alone cool-ass rock star women.)

Asking Kevin about the title, he sighs and pauses for a while before getting more oblique than usual. "The word 'love' is very powerful even when you put anything after it. It's difficult to explain, but it's to do with effect and feel and to have some tangible meaning, with the meaning being less important than the overall effect." It's clear that it still is hard to talk about, and I don't blame him. Kevin does allow that "it would be basically true to say that the lyrics were as much about us as anything, but they weren't completely 'cause as I said there were these other issues that were influencing us. So, her lyrics and my lyrics would be that kind of thing as well."

Asked whether the album's title referred to their relationship, Bilinda replies, "I think it did, in a way, but it was not just us. You know, I think he found the whole process of making *Loveless*, in the end, just such a slog. The songs were so brilliant, and I think the state Kevin had to get into to create those was compromised by just a lot of misery going on around us, nothing particularly terrible happening to anybody, but it was kind of a depressing time. I was not the most bubbling, happy person, you know."

At the time, the two never spoke about their relationship status to the press. "The media here in England are extremely tabloidish—the *NME*, you know what I mean?," Kevin says. "You just don't want to give them anything 'cause everything's an *issue*, so you just say as little as possible really and you get away with it then. What I learned is that you can be as private as you want really, unless you're really famous. But if you're in a position like me, you can have your privacy; you have to just make it happen."

Bilinda's voice brightens considerably as she describes first crushing out on her band mate. "He just seemed really gentle, a really soft-spoken, gentle guy, a bit geeky," she says. "He had these glasses that were always done up with cellotape [*laughs*] and always seemed to wear the same clothes all the time, which I used to do too then, so it really wasn't so unusual. He always had his stripey shirts and a leather jacket, sort of a bomber jacket, and this black jumper that became legendary. It had what started as a tiny hole that probably came from dropping a bit of burning cigarette or something, and then it just ended up in this massive big hole but he still used to wear it, you know. So, he was scruffy, but adorable." "I never wore a bomber jacket in my life; it's amazing that's what she remembers!" Kevin interjects.

When Bilinda joined the band she was having "a bit of a hard time" with the father of her son Toby. "We were sort of together but he was being quite violent and things were going really wrong. He was becoming quite suicidal, and telling Toby that he was gonna kill himself and all this. So there was this whole scenario going on when I first joined the band. And Toby's dad wasn't too happy that I got the audition, even though he latched me up with going to it. He wasn't jealous at first, 'cause he knew that doing backing vocals wasn't really what he wanted to do. But I started playing guitar—and he was a guitarist, and I had never picked up his guitar at home or anything—and now I was suddenly playing guitar. There was a bit of, you know, animosity." Kevin and Bilinda didn't really start going out until six months or a year after she joined.

"We were together properly from '88 till '92," Kevin says. "I mean, it's complicated you know. She was living in the house until '97; we were together on and off for more than ten years. Those two records are a real document of that, in a way—our coming together made that [music] happen, even though I would be 'in charge' of everything musically. I was the leader of the band and everything. But Bilinda, when she joined the band, she brought very good taste in music, and this sort of energy, for want of a better word, and atmosphere."

Bilinda says her relationship with Kevin "was brilliant in the beginning—best thing in the world—but when we did *Loveless*, things were falling apart. But he was always off, and during *Loveless*, the hours were so upside-down. He'd be in the studio all day. And sometimes I would be there too, but I had to be there for Toby [in the day]. There was a yearning feeling, you know. We were living together but not really being together. And, um, a lot of times we weren't really like a proper couple anymore, and we weren't sure if we were going to split up or get back together, you know? We did split up when we went on the tour after *Loveless*; we sort of split up on the week of our first gig. We went to Australia first, and we decided that would be it."

"It was just quicker and easier to live together, and we always thought we would get back together, maybe," Bilinda says. "I was going through my own personal nightmares and I think we were also smoking too much dope. I still really cared about Kevin, even though I knew we couldn't be together, and I think we'll never really stop caring about each other in that way. We really loved each other, but we tend to just push each other's buttons, and being trapped together for the longest time on tour [is not easy]. It was a weird thing, because although we'd have all these big fights, we still always got on together. The only time we really fell out for a time was when I moved out of the house, you know. I think Kevin felt a bit abandoned by everybody then; he was just left having to keep it still going. And I didn't leave because I wanted to leave the band, I just felt like I was the one who needed to sort myself out. It was hard 'cause I felt like there wasn't any connection at all, you know, and I felt really sad. Really, really sad."

Chapter Fifteen
Blown a Wish

When Shields started work on the album in late 1989, the Berlin Wall was still standing, Nelson Mandela had not yet been set free. And the Gulf War—which Shields and crew watched on TV inside Protocol studios—had yet to happen. *Loveless* was released on November 4, 1991, within a year of Nirvana's *Nevermind*, Massive Attack's *Blue Lines*, Pavement's *Slanted & Enchanted*, the Orb's *Adventures Beyond the Ultraworld* and Cypress Hill's debut. It never charted in the US, and peaked at number twenty-four on the UK albums chart.

For the most part, consensus was unanimous on *Loveless*. There were minor quibbles, usually from writers who wanted it to be more "electronic," but even those reservations were voiced from inside glowing reviews. Giving the record an A-, American critic Robert Christgau wrote that "Some may cringe at the grotesque distortions they extract from their guitars, others at the soprano murmurs that provide theoretical relief. I didn't much go for either myself. But after suitable suffering and peer support, I learned. In the destructive elements immerse."

There have been *Loveless* detractors, of course, notably critic Chuck Eddy, who considers the band one of the ten worst of all time. In his 1997 collection *The Accidental Evolution of Rock'N'Roll: A Misguided Tour Through Popular Music*, the former *Village Voice* music editor refers to "such British hypes as My Bloody Valentine who were trying to treat 'dream pop' as an end in itself, having heard Suicide's 'Dream Baby Dream' once and having thereby determined deadweight vocals sound menacing and new-age drones equal art." I'd love to see concrete criticism of the band, but Eddy seems to have as much a problem with the band themselves as the critics who gush about them so. One feels that perhaps they are being faulted simply for being hyped by others.

In another *Accidental* passage, Eddy rails that "social-tranquilizer cult acts like My Bloody Valentine codify old Byrds and Velvet Underground moves into sexless obviousness, call it 'mystic,' and are embraced by critics who are in turn inspired to write with a lethargy that mimics the music; nobody ever cranks out reviews saying 'these My Bloody Valentine songs kick butt, but these turds over here totally bite the oceanic big one.'" There is a valid point in

there, but it strikes me as a bit like deciding you hate Neil
Young because his fans are total dorks. I don't recall MBV
ever calling their own music "mystic," either; they may be
Irish but they're not U2. Speaking of that sort of rubbish,
the *NME* review of the album states that "however deca-
dent one might find the idea of elevating other human
beings to deities, My Bloody Valentine, failings and all,
deserve more than your respect."

And so it is with most reviews of the album:
Translucent. Genius. Shimmering. Genius. Glorious.
Genius. Beautiful. Etc. It's hard to think of a superlative
that hasn't been showered its way at one point or another.
And of course, when you pile that much praise so high up
into the sky, it inevitably reads as impossible hype. The
album has become a cliché in the sense that it's ultimate fan
boy pinnacle of everything, spoken of with hushed whis-
pers. On any given day, there seems to be a new thread
about *Loveless* on *I Love Music*, the excellent online commu-
nity/message board for besotted music geeks, which
inevitably generates dozens of responses. Pitchfork has
called it the second best album of the 90s, while it's ranked
number 219 on *Rolling Stone* magazine's list of the 500
greatest records of all time.

Chapter Sixteen
We Have All the Time in the World

I was initially going to end the book with the release of the album, and the critical response to it. But what happened after *Loveless* is, at this point, as much a part of the story as what led up to it. And even after Shields started giving interviews again after the release of the *Lost in Translation* soundtrack in 2003 that he contributed to, much of this period remains misunderstood.

After parting ways with Creation, the band signed to Island Records in October of 1992. A nice-sized advance in hand, Shields arranged for a studio to be built inside a house in Streatham and everything was in place by April of 1993. But the mixing desk didn't work. A brand new unit, it had been built faultily. And by the time people figured out what was wrong, thousands of pounds and months of effort had been wasted, the group went into "semi-meltdown," as

Shields told *Buddyhead*. "We had come back from tour, done the deal, built the studio, and then the studio didn't work, so then we ended up fighting the record company over the fact that they never wanted us to build the studio in the first place," he explained. "They thought it was dangerous. We had been given 250,000 pounds, and by the time we had finished building the studio and everything, we had nothing left, and no studio."

As Colm and Kevin set about making the follow-up to *Loveless*, it was clearly going to be influenced by the drum and bass music the two had gotten into from its being played on pirate radio stations and in underground clubs. "We had really a strong base for a while and in our heads were taking [our music] to another level. But of course we weren't, really. It was just a long process of trying to figure out what [drum and bass] was and again doing it our own way. Then we realized that it's actually quite simple music if you use the right samples and stuff. We would play a version of it that was slower, a more jazzy version, which at the time seemed very radical. That just seemed natural. Now, it's the most mainstream thing; no one would think twice about it. We were trying to make the rhythms of the guitars and the rhythm of the drums go together so it was this kind of big organic creature." Will people ever be able to hear this stuff or did it all get scrapped? "Largely scrapped," Kevin says. "The concept was large and that concept is gone."

"[With *Loveless*] it was such a long process moving from

studio to studio," Bilinda says. "It felt like a jinx, like it was just such a slog to get anything done properly. And when we bought a studio, we thought 'This will solve all that,' and then all that happened with the mixing board. Even still, lots of stuff did get done in the studio. Colm was in charge of learning to use the computer. There were always a lot of great sounds coming out when you'd be having tea downstairs. Every day there I'd be thinking 'Oh, I'll be going in to do some vocals soon,' and I never did, except for the Wire track and the Louis Armstrong thing. But that was it."

In several interviews, McGee has painted Shields as totally bonkers during the time he had the home studio, with an entire room overrun by chinchillas and sandbags barricading them in. The sandbags were actually there to soundproof the studio. "There are stories and theories that Kevin went mad while we were at the house and at the time we were all falling out [with each other]," Bilinda says. "He was very difficult to be around, but he was dealing with the record people from day to day, and then he'd be trying to keep the finances for the whole house going, paying engineers, keeping the mortgage paid, and so on. I don't know how he managed to keep the house going; it should have been bankrupted years before it was. He had this amazing ability to keep things going."

The chinchilla thing, however, is totally true. Kevin and Bilinda had a full-on chinchilla problem. Bilinda recalls that they had as many as twenty of the critters at once, but Kevin goes to pains to point out that fourteen chinchillas was the max (because, of course, twenty chinchillas is crazy but fourteen is nothing at all). "They all lived in this big room together, and the boys were separately from the girls," Bilinda laughs. "I had a very beautiful pedigreed chinchilla, and her husband was from a pet shop—he was actually the one who sort of set the whole chinchilla thing off, his name was Softy. It was quite funny because he was quite the opposite; he used to come and nibble your ankles and was a bit vicious, but from being pent up, you know? Chinchillas are really very cute, and they're sort of like a cross between a rabbit and a squirrel, and they've got the softest fur in the world. And they're very dexterous with their hands; they hold their food and they look like they're just eating a sandwich, you know, very dainty."

I had planned to write a chapter that would serve as a mini-manifesto for why bands should feel fine not making another record, especially if they've made the best one of their careers already. I read a lovely little book, *Bartleby & Co.*, by Enrique Vila-Matas, which is a meditation on writers who do not write, or who stop writing. The book talks about authors such as Robert Walser, who famously said, "I'm not here to write, but to be mad!" to an old friend visiting at the asylum he'd checked himself into years earlier. Then I realized that, while he's certainly been out of the public eye and no one would call him prolific, Shields is no Bartleby. The guy has been quite busy, scoring music for dances, collaborating with Patti Smith, making music that no one else hears, playing what you might call sound effects guitar in Primal Scream, and recording some new stuff for the *Lost in Translation* movie. He continues to make much of his living through production work—remixes, mostly. He's done wonderful remixes for the Go Team!, Yo La Tengo, Mogwai and Placebo.

Asked about the possibilities of a solo record, Kevin alludes to some of why he's been in a holding pattern for a while now, he says yes, but allows that he needs to make some changes first, to learn to just say "no." "I had a disastrous couple of years where I took on loads of stuff and I wound up doing nothing properly. I did lots of touring with Primal Scream doing all these things in the middle which took too long. And I was working on another band's album for six months and then the band broke up. So I learned that if it's not your own stuff you shouldn't really pull people through the hedges. Perhaps give people a helping hand, but if you have to actually drag them for six months of your life, it probably shouldn't really be happening."

Colm O'Ciosoig formed a group called the Warm Inventions in 2000 with Hope Sandoval from Mazzy Star. They've released two EPs and one album together. Colm also worked closely with Andy Cabic on the first and self-titled Vetiver album from 2003, a pastoral folk-rock record, and he recorded with British folk guitar legend Bert Jansch in 2002.

Bilinda is busy raising her two sons and recently passed

her exams to teach Spanish dance professionally. She's just starting to sing again for the first time in a dozen years. Together with her partner Eugene (son of deceased singer-songwriter Kevin Coyne) she's recorded one of Kevin's songs for a tribute album. And it's clear that she feels things are unresolved for MBV. "I'll never feel satisfied, 'cause I have a yearning for us to do something still. That's the thing about moving into that house; that music never happened, and it was meant to. It's got to be resolved one day."

Deb relates that her band Snowpony (who released albums in 1998 and 2001) are still together, "although we haven't done anything for ages." The group recorded six tracks for their next album "about a year ago, but haven't got around to doing the rest of them. I guess we all have other priorities at the moment." She's also involved in a women's drag king collective called Joybabe. "We get together occasionally, put on shows that usually involve dragging up, play covers and raising money." As to the prospects of a reunion, "if it follows the same time span as *Loveless* and the last album (that never was), it's going to be quite a while yet. I'm not sure how enthralling the idea of an octogenarian MBV is really."

Kevin swears that the band members are still close friends and could work again together soon. "First I have to make the solo record; that will give us the money to make the My Bloody Valentine record the way we want to make it," he says. Vinita Joshi relays that Kevin will likely soon remaster the older tracks [for the long-delayed EP collection for Sony]. "And we now have the rights to the domain name mybloodyvalentine.co.uk; we are talking to Debbie about getting this up and running." On the reunion question, she cryptically answers, "How can there be a reunion when they have never disbanded? You can expect new Kevin material and MBV material in the future. Time is only a creation by the mind."

Chapter Seventeen
What You Want

"I think the only problem I have now, and maybe it's fix-able, is the very ending of the book," my editor David Barker writes. "Is there not some way to make it slightly more upbeat? In a weird way, the message at the end of this book could be: 'If you're stubborn enough, and cre-ative enough, and don't give in to the endless demands of the Man (or Alan McGee), then you really can end up with a record that, 15 years on, sells enough copies every week to keep you comfortable so you can carry on doing exact-ly what you want, at the pace you want to, etc etc . . . ' I just kind of like the idea that Shields today has some limited artistic and financial freedom, which seems like a just reward for the hell he went through, trying to get this record made in the way he wanted it made."

I know this is a short book. But it's taken some time to

complete, and I'm super tempted to just write "what he said" here and be done with it. But I'll try to address my editor's concerns with as little finesse as possible. For me, the power of the album itself is enough. I don't need a sequel, and don't want one. It really seems like Kevin's going to make and release some new music in the next decade and it's going to be far better than the few tunes on the *Lost in Translation* soundtrack. Of course, it's not really Kevin's fault that his songs for *Translation* aren't super stellar. As he told *Buddyhead*, "They gave me the opportunity to replace some of the music they had in the rough cuts. But it had to be a similar style of what was already there, which was an imitation of My Bloody Valentine. So it was a little weird trying to imitate something that was trying to imitate something I had done before." That must have been a very strange position to be in, to copy someone copying you, but Shields definitely made some decent money from that soundtrack work. Hopefully it will lead to more of the same for him.

They might have been having trouble toward the end of their relationship, but today, Kevin and Bilinda sound a lot closer than I am with any of my exes. They see each other at all the major holidays, as well as out at gigs and such. Bilinda talked about crying during Kevin's backup performance to Patti Smith's "Coral Sea" piece on June 22, 2005. I spoke to both of them just after Christmas 2005; Bilinda had gotten Kevin a handful of awesome bootleg

Ramones DVDs and both were enthusing about the things. Debbie was clearly joking about how Colm was never available for comment for the book, and I just figure he wants to get on with his life, to put *Loveless* behind him. I was probably the six hundredth dork trying to track him down to discuss a record he hardly plays on anyway.

Loveless is more than influential; it's a record musicians and listeners alike project themselves on to with great force. Pitchfork refers to an album by Noxagt as "*Loveless*-style noisemaking"; it's now its own genre. Alan McGee raves that an album by Mogwai is "possibly better than *Loveless*." All Music Guide calls Glifted's album *Under and In* "some of the most impressive post-*Loveless* rock in years," as if we all understand there are two eras in music now: BL and AL. Pitchfork worries itself into a state of near-entropy over the disc: "Is there anything new that can possibly be said about *Loveless*? Any stone as yet unturned?" Vinita says simply: "I think the record is timeless (like Nick Drake) and was so ahead of its time. I still play it now regularly; I hear different things all the time. Maybe I connect with different layers, or it's me listening in a different state of mind."

The only writing about *Loveless* that bothers me comes in the guise of folks purporting that Shields was some sort of crazy slacker, an accidental genius at best. I've done my best to avoid using "the g word," myself anyway, just as I've not compared him once to Brian Wilson in the entire course of the book. But the more one researches the making of *Loveless*, the more it becomes clear that Shields had these amazing sounds in his head, that he knew almost exactly how he wanted to get them down. And while he obviously wasn't the easiest guy to deal with if you happened to work for a label or studio, it seems that hardly anyone trusted Shields enough to furnish him with the proper tools to realize that very specific and otherworldly vision.

Such intense devotion to one's own vision is by turns quixotic and almost spiritual. I just find it life-affirming as hell, myself; if you make a TV documentary about *Loveless*, perhaps it should be for the Lifetime network, not VH-1. The spiritual side to this album is something Vinita and I scribble back and forth to each other about regularly. "Not only are MBV out of this world, they follow no rules. What they do is new and refreshing and created in a different way to any other music. The layers, the texturing, you can get lost in it. To me all music is spiritual. It's been proven to be good for the soul. Even the gurus in India suggest some mellow music before bedtime to end the day; the soul is nourished and by nourishing the soul you are experiencing higher levels of spirituality."

Postscript
Wave Field

As deferred expectations go, the use of My Bloody Valentine as a critical reference point is worse even than a first date with someone you've met online, or getting all psyched about a politician before they actually take office: such expectations are nearly impossible to live up to. I mean Christ, the fact remains that My Bloody Valentine themselves couldn't follow up *Loveless*—so how could anyone else?

I have on multiple occasions found myself worked up over acts referred to generically in reviews as "MBV-ish," among them decent indie rock acts like Mogwai and M83 and Part Chimp and Guitar and Sigur Rós. I would read a glowing review that spoke of "ethereal guitar textures à la MBV," or whatever, and send in my money, ultimately realizing I'd gotten my hopes all up for . . . not that much. I might as well have been ordering copies of *Grit* from the back of a comic book to sell door-to-door. There are a few exceptions, thankfully, each of them coming less from the rock side of things and more from a fucked-up electronic/droney bent, notably AMP, Black Dice, Flowchart, William Basinski, Nudge and Caribou (formerly Manitoba).

And MBV's influence on electronic music continues unabated. The "Instrumental A"/"Instrumental B" seven-inch included with the first copies of 1988's *Isn't Anything* seemed to point toward the gritty sounds of early jungle and darkwave, which began to appear four or five years later. Now, I doubt that obscure little record was much of a direct influence on the genre's development. But the self-sampled and deliberately smeared sounding textural elements of *Loveless* undoubtedly (and in some cases very obviously) influenced much of the best ambient electronic music from the 90s and the 00s, including Viennese guitarist and laptopist Christian Fennesz, the gorgeous minimalist house music of Germany's Isolée, German software-based musician Markus Popp and the Portuguese guitarist Rafael Toral.

In 1995, less than four years after the release of *Loveless*, the then-unknown Toral released an LP with three pieces on it on a tiny local label. *Wave Field* was explicitly an homage to *Loveless*, with a cover that mimics the original—a blurry color-saturated photo of the Fender Jaguar with which Toral made his album. Hypnotic and dizzying, the album is a wonderful accompaniment to *Loveless*. To stick with 90s metaphors, if *Loveless* is the best warehouse rave you ever went to, *Wave Field* is the "chillout room" at that rave.

Resounding frequencies overlap and gyrate, wiggling their way inside your body. The notes, tones and clusters of guitar-induced and effects-generated sounds reverberate amongst each other. In a review at the time, I wrote that "it almost sounds underwater: if whales used guitars and electronics to sing to one another, it might sound like this," unaware of how many reviewers had compared the sounds on *Loveless* to whale calls, especially on Colm's weird, short song "Touched." I enthusiastically added in my review of the album that "*Wave Field* is an astonishing, left-field work, a drone fan's dream. It's everything you wanted from Fripp & Eno's *No Pussyfooting* and Spacemen 3's *Dreamweapon* & very nearly got: full, dynamic layers of blissful, amp-moaning pleasure-noise that ebbs and flows like the sea." Listening to it for the first time in years, I am only slightly less effusive in my praise. Like *Loveless*, it's aged really well. Unlike it, the album has slid into obscurity, and, as of this writing, is out of print.

I interviewed Rafael Toral upon the record's release in 1998 on Dexter's Cigar (a short-lived reissue label operated by Jim O'Rourke and David Grubbs in the last year that their band Gastr del Sol was together). "I wanted to make an ambient piece that sounded like a thousand rock gigs reverberating from a distant hall," he explained, writing from his home/recording studio in Lisbon, located on the same street he grew up. "It's a distillation of rock music, as if one could squeeze the juice, and make it liquid, a flowing essence." *Wave Field* utilized "materials and textures from rock, based on its dearest icon, the electric guitar. I aimed at an ambient record charged with the resonance and the dirt and noise of rock music." Rock music, per se, isn't the goal, but rather rock's essential "energy, electricity, intensity. Everything I developed in ten years of work with the guitar is here."

One of the things that made *Wave Field* special to Toral, who at the time called it his "masterpiece," is what he referred to as its "two faces." The words "play very soft or very loud" are printed on the insert. "When it's played loud it becomes something completely different: a very physical, hypnotizing wave of electric drone that you feel around your body—like a river," he explained. Bill Meyer, the first American writer to draw attention to Toral's talents (though Toral was initially "discovered" here by minimalist composer Phill Niblock), elaborated on the guitarist's processes and playing styles to me in an email: "He liberally uses an e-bow and delays to get sustained sounds, and he uses a guitar synth on *Wave Field*. I've seen him balance a toy Marshall amp on the guitar's neck to get a Buck Rogers laser gun. He's really into air and space travel; his other album covers feature airplanes, and he performs *Wave Field* accompanied by homemade films of planes taking off and landing."

All the sounds on *Wave Field* were made with just one Fender Jaguar. "It's basically tapping the guitar without touching the strings and working with resonant frequencies, using filters and equalizers, then some reverb," he explained. "I recorded two sets of resonant drones in a weekend and that became the base for the piece. I later added loops, tones and percussion sounds—all with the guitar—and gradually composed the piece from there. I'd lay sounds in the digital tracks and remove the ones that were redundant or unnecessary."

The funny thing is that Toral's method for composing *Wave Field* was exactly the way so many people mistakenly think that Shields himself works: obsessively laboring over every microsecond, spending as much time removing sounds as adding them. Toral used DAT tape and his computer to store, layer, and edit the work. It took a year to complete *Wave Field*, everything done in-studio, right up to the mastering. The '98 reissue saw the eradication of a few mistakes "that nobody else could hear," ironed out to Toral's compulsive satisfaction. "The result is a more perfect wholeness," he said. Unlike with MBV, there were no supposed chicken-eating contests or days in an expensive studio spent watching television waiting for the muse to hit, but of course at the time Toral hadn't seen legions of bands formed simply to ape his own sound, and the entire British press hadn't called Toral a "genius" repeatedly. No one, in fact, seemed aware of Toral outside Portugal.

The decision to make an album so explicitly in defer-ence/reference to one that had come out a few years earli-er and had instantly been deified is a curious one. But Toral has always had an "oh-thank-you-but-so-and-so-did-it-first-and-all-the-credit-should-go-to-them" manner. We've been email pals for years and he's genuinely a humble guy, and in that way he's like Shields himself. Toral's one of those artists who liberally, excitedly points to his own influences (which also include Alvin Lucier, Nuno Canavarro, Brian Eno, and Sonic Youth), at times giving them more credit than they might deserve.

And it is more than mere humility. Toral demonstrates actual insight into these artists' work. He once told me that that he enjoys "to be inspired or influenced by someone on a conceptual level, rather than on a formal one. That's why you can be highly inspired by someone but then you won't sound like an imitation of it, you can go in any direction when it comes to formal thinking. In other words, the same thoughts can be expressed in a variety of ways."

When Toral discussed *Loveless* with me, he said that he thought Kevin Shields's "greatest breakthrough was the production techniques he used, especially on that record. The immersive sound he created has no precedent! Another thing very unique about My Bloody Valentine is the blend of ethereal ambience with a very intense sensu-ality, together with this kind of raw harshness, a certain violence," a sentiment I obviously concur with. He ended by saying that "the entire 'shoegazing' generation which followed totally missed the point," something with which it's also highly difficult to disagree.